FG–E–5.9
APRIL 1963

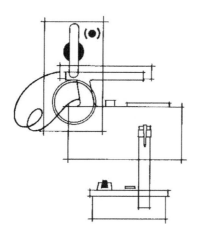

HANDBOOK
FOR
RADIOLOGICAL
MONITORS

**DEPARTMENT OF DEFENSE
OFFICE OF CIVIL DEFENSE**

FOREWORD

This handbook has been prepared for use by radiological monitors in community shelters and at fallout monitoring stations. It provides basic information the monitor must have to carry out his duties of detection, measurement, and reporting of radiation. While it is primarily intended for use as an operations manual in conducting radiological monitoring, it is also intended for use as a student manual in monitor training. Additional copies may be obtained through your local civil defense organization by citing the title and the Federal Civil Defense Guide number, FG-E-5.9.

TABLE OF CONTENTS

ii

I. INTRODUCTION

1.1 Radiological monitoring is an indispensable service to all civil defense organizations and their operations. In the event of a nuclear attack, trained monitors will be required to furnish information essential for the protection of people. Monitoring services will be required from the period shortly after a nuclear attack until the radiological hazard from fallout diminishes to the point that normal activities may be resumed without significant danger to the population of a community.

Purpose

1.2 This handbook provides the radiological monitor with the information and techniques normally required to perform essential duties. It also provides guidance that may be required, *but should not be used*, unless competent guidance is unavailable from a radiological defense officer. The possession of this manual is not sufficient to assure that an untrained person can effectively carry out the duties and responsibilities required of a radiological monitor. All personnel assigned monitoring responsibilities should complete, as a minimum, the Radiological Monitoring Course prescribed by the Office of Civil Defense, Department of Defense.

Scope

1.3 The radiological monitor will perform his duties under a variety of conditions. This handbook furnishes him with information concerning the techniques and procedures to be followed, the protective measures that should be taken, and the application of these techniques and procedures to the various types of monitoring operations that are required.

Monitoring System

1.4 The radiological defense information necessary to support post-attack civil defense operations requires a minimum nationwide network of 150,000 fallout monitoring stations. In addition, since designated group or public shelters will be strong points of survival from which people will emerge to carry out recovery and rehabilitation, each shelter must have a capability to perform monitoring for the safety of shelter occupants. If the group or public shelters provide appropriate geographic and communications coverage, some will probably be chosen as locations for fallout monitoring stations.

1.5 Fallout station monitors provide the primary information for conducting radiological defense operations. It is expected that monitors in these stations will receive technical direction and supervision from their organizational Radiological Defense Officer. Shelter monitors provide at each shelter an independent means of limiting the radiation exposure of shelter occupants. Following the shelter period, both fallout station monitors and shelter monitors will be required to support recovery operations.

Requirements for Monitoring

1.6 During the early post-attack period when people are in shelter, most monitoring will be performed from fallout monitoring stations and from shelters. The radiological information needed by shelter occupants, and by the Federal, State and local governments for survival activities, will require monitoring of personnel, food and water, and monitoring of areas-in-shelter and possibly out-of-shelter. Aerial monitoring may be required for rapid survey of large areas or specific transportation routes. When dose rates have decreased to the extent that limited outside activities can be performed, some shelter monitors and probably all fallout station monitors will become mobile and will support operations of emergency services such as fire, police or rescue.

1.7 There is a continuing need for monitoring through the period of gradual relaxation of sheltered living even after gamma radiation no longer seriously restricts unsheltered living. During the recovery period, the need for frequent reports of monitored data becomes less urgent but the requirement for monitoring of specific areas, facilities, personnel and equipment, food and water, and monitoring in support of large-scale decontamination operations increases. Monitoring is required until all radiation hazards are determined to be insignificant.

1.8 Aerial monitoring, which may be required during the early post-attack period for rapid survey of large areas, is covered in a separate publication. Aerial monitors should be chosen from among the best qualified monitors and should receive special training in this technique.

Duties and Responsibilities

1.9 The primary duty of a radiological monitor is to provide timely and accurate information required for the proper analysis and evaluation of the radiological hazard. Whether the monitor is assigned to a fallout monitoring station or to a shelter, which may also be designated as a fallout monitoring station, he must know and be able to do the following:

a. Follow the monitoring SOP (Standing Operating Procedure) established by the organization to which he is assigned. This will require an understanding of his function in the plan, the conditions that require monitoring, when and how to report radiation measurements, and how to maintain required records. If no local SOP exists, follow the procedures in section V of this handbook.

b. Know the types, uses, and operation of all OCD radiological instruments and related equipment discussed in this handbook.

c. Use the monitoring techniques required both during and following shelter occupancy. These techniques will include surface, personnel, food and water monitoring and monitoring in support of emergency operations.

d. Carry out the protective measures necessary to keep personnel exposures to a minimum.

1.10 The above knowledges and skills will enable the trained monitor to perform tasks such as the following:

a. Measure the gamma exposure dose of shelter occupants.

b. Monitor levels of radiation inside shelters to locate best shielded areas for use when dose rates are high, and to locate other acceptable areas in the building where shelter areas are located to permit greater freedom of movement and improve living conditions of shelter occupants after dose rates have decreased.

c. Monitor unsheltered levels of radiation at fallout monitoring stations to provide radiological information for emergency operations.

d. Monitor to obtain additional supplies and to recover vital installations at the earliest practicable time.

e. Monitor routes needed for remedial movement and for transportation in general.

f. Monitor in support of emergency operations to accomplish decontamination and recovery activities.

II. RADIOLOGICAL INSTRUMENTS

2.1 OCD has developed several radiological instruments which together provide a wide monitoring capability. All of these instruments are designed to detect and measure gamma radiation. Some have the additional capability of detecting beta radiation, but none are designed to detect or measure alpha radiation.

2.2 Instruments for radiological defense operations can be divided generally into two classes: (1) *survey meters* for measuring gamma dose rates in roentgens per hour (r/hr) or milliroentgens per hour (mr/hr), and (2) *dosimeters* for measuring exposure doses in roentgens (r).

2.3 The uses and operating characteristics of each civil defense instrument are discussed in succeeding pages. A monitor must be thoroughly familiar with each of these instruments. Several characteristics common to all instruments are discussed beginning with paragraph 2.19.

CD V-700

2.4 *Uses.*—The CD V-700, 0–50 mr/hr survey meter, is a low range instrument that measures gamma dose rates and detects the presence of beta. It can be used (1) in long term clean-up and decontamination operations, (2) for personnel monitoring, and (3) for indicating the degree of radioactive contamination in food and water.

The CD V-700 is designed for low level measurements and has limited usefulness in areas of high contamination.

2.5 When the probe shield on the CD V-700 is closed, beta is stopped and only the gamma dose rate is measured. When the shield is open, both beta and gamma are detected. However, the difference in the unshielded reading and the shielded reading, which represents the beta contribution, can be interpreted only in a general way by qualified radiological personnel.

2.6 If an audible indication is desired, a headphone may be attached to the connector at the lower left corner of the instrument cover. The c/m scale on the meter should be disregarded by the monitor.

2.7 *Controls.*—There is only one control on the CD V-700. This control, a selector switch, can be moved to the OFF position and three ranges labeled ×100 (times 100), ×10 (times 10), and ×1 (times 1). On the ×1 range, the measured dose rate is read directly from the meter. On the ×10 and ×100 ranges, the meter readings must be multiplied by 10 and 100 respectively to obtain the measured dose rate.

4

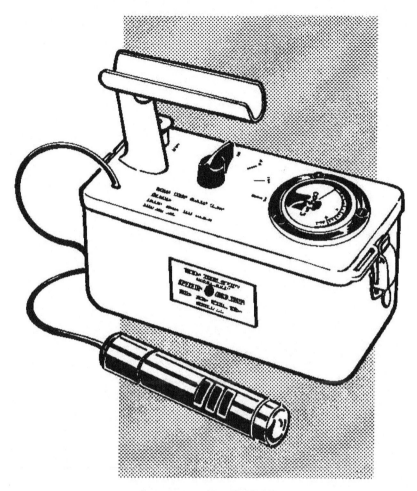

2.8 *Operational Check.*—Prior to use, the CD V-700 should be checked to assure that it is operating properly. The "operational check" should be performed in a radiation free area as follows: (1) turn the selector switch to the ×10 range and allow at least 30 seconds for warm up, (2) rotate the shield on the probe to the fully open position, and (3) place the open area of the probe as close as possible to the operational check source located on the instrument case. The meter should read between 1.5 and 2.5 mr/hr. If the reading is not within this interval and if the CD V-700 has been recently calibrated, the reading from the check source should be noted. This reading should remain the same during future operational checks.

2.9 The operational check source should be used to determine that the CD V-700 is operating properly. Its use does not replace the need for calibrating the instrument. During an emergency, the presence of external

5

radiation from fallout may prohibit the performance of an operational check. In this event, the monitor should assume a calibrated CD V 700 is operating properly if it indicates radiation levels above normal background.

2.10 *Jamming.*—One particular operating characteristic of the CD V–700 with which the monitor should be familiar is "jamming" or "saturation." Radiation dose rates from 50 mr/hr to 1 r/hr will produce off-scale readings. However, when dose rates materially exceed 1 r/hr, the CD V–700 may "jam" or "saturate" and read zero or less than full scale. A higher range instrument is required for measurement of dose rates higher than 50 mr/hr.

CD V–715

2.11 *Uses.*—The CD V–715, 0-500 r/hr survey meter, will measure gamma dose rates only and is used for general post-attack operations. It is designed (1) for ground survey, (2) for use in fallout monitoring stations and community shelters, and (3) as an interim aerial survey instrument.

ILLUSTRATION 2.11—CD V–715.

It will be used by the monitor for the major portion of survey requirements in the period immediately following a nuclear weapon attack. The CD V–715 has no beta detection capability.

2.12 *Controls.*—Two controls are provided on the CD V–715. One control, a selector switch has seven positions: CIRCUIT CHECK, OFF, ZERO, and ×100 (times 100), ×10 (times 10), ×1 (times 1) and ×0.1 (times 0.1) ranges. On the ×1 range, the measured dose rate is read directly from the meter. On the ×0.1, ×10, and ×100 ranges, the meter readings must be multiplied by a factor of 0.1, 10, or 100 respectively in order to obtain the measured dose rate. A second control, the zero control, is used to adjust the meter reading to zero during the operational check, and to adjust for "zero drift" during long periods of operation.

2.13 *Operational Check.*—Prior to use, the CD V–715 should be checked to assure that it is operating properly. The "operational check" is performed as follows: (1) turn the selector switch to the ZERO position, allow at least two minutes for warm up, and adjust the zero control to make the meter read zero, (2) turn the selector switch to the CIRCUIT CHECK position, (the meter should read within the red band marked "circuit check"), (3) recheck the zero setting as the selector switch is turned to the four ranges: ×100, ×10, ×1, and ×0.1. When only normal background radiation is present, the meter should read not more than two scale divisions upscale on any range.

2.14 *Modification (CD V–717).*—Some of the CD V–715's will be equipped by the manufacturer with a removable ionization chamber attached to 25 feet of cable. This modification, called the CD V–717, will provide a remote reading capability for the fallout monitoring stations. The operating characteristics are identical to the CD V–715, except that the removable ionization chamber may be placed outside the shelter in an unshielded area and protected from possible contamination by placing it in a bag or cover of light-weight material. Readings may then be observed from within the fallout monitoring station. After the early period of high fallout radiation dose rates, and the requirement for a remote reading instrument diminishes, the removable ionization chamber should be checked for contamination with the CD V–700; decontaminated, if necessary, and returned to the case. The CD V–717 may then be used for other monitoring operations.

CD V–742

2.15 *Uses.*—The CD V–742, 0–200r dosimeter, is designed for measuring accumulated exposure doses of gamma radiation to operations personnel and shelter occupants. It can be read by holding it toward any light source sufficient to see the scale and hairline.

2.16 *Initial Check.*—There is no "operational check" for dosimeters similar to the check for survey meters. However, when dosimeters are received, the monitor should zero them, and check their electrical leakage characteristics. The leakage characteristics may be checked by zeroing the dosimeters and placing them in a radiation free area for 4 days. If the

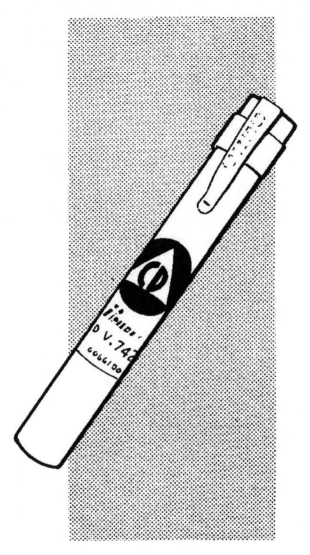

ILLUSTRATION 2.15—CD V-742.

leakage rate exceeds 5% of full scale per 4 days, the dosimeters should not be used provided other dosimeters are available. If no other dosimeters are available, the leakage rate should be determined and the contribution from electrical leakage subtracted from the dose as measured by the leaking dosimeter.

2.17 *Storage.*—Most civil defense dosimeters will require a "soak in" charge after long-term storage in an uncharged condition. Consequently, such dosimeters should be charged and the reading observed for a few hours before using them. A second charging may be required before the dosim-

8

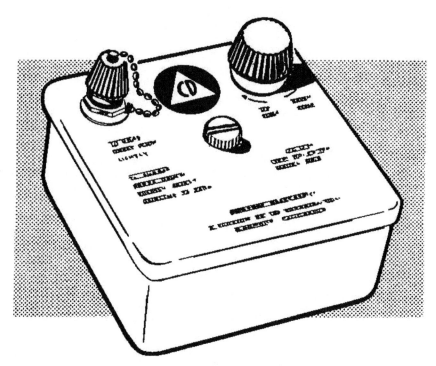

ILLUSTRATION 2.18—CD V-750.

eters are ready for use. When not in use, dosimeters should be *charged* and stored in a *dry* place. When performing scheduled checks of instruments, dosimeters should be read and if they indicate more than one-fourth of full scale, they should be recharged to zero.

CD V-750

2.18 *Uses.*—The CD V-750, dosimeter charger, is used to charge (zero) and read civil defense dosimeters. Instructions for charging dosimeters are printed on each charger. If no light source is available, a dosimeter may be read on a charger as follows: (1) remove the dust cover from the charging receptacle, (2) place the dosimeter on the charging contact, and (3) press lightly to light the lamp. Do not press firmly, since the hairline may change position if the charging switch is closed.

Characteristics Common to All Instruments

2.19 *Batteries.*—Refer to the manufacturer's instruction manual for the proper battery installation procedure. Particular attention should be given to correct battery polarity during installation. For instruments subject to intermittent use, batteries should be removed monthly and the battery contacts inspected for any dirt or corrosion present. Dirty contacts should be cleaned. If the instrument is to be stored for more than one week, batteries should be *removed* from the instrument and stored in a cool dry

9

place. Whenever an instrument is not in use, *make certain that it is turned off;* otherwise, the batteries will be discharged and the instrument rendered ineffective and/or permanently damaged by battery leakage. With good batteries, all instruments should operate continuously for 100–150 hours. Intermittent use should extend the operating life two or three times.

2.20 *Calibration.*—Each instrument should be calibrated annually or in accordance with the local calibration schedule. Although the monitor may be requested to inform the RADEF officer or other civil defense official when instruments are due for calibration, he is not responsible for assuring that it is done. The monitor *must not* attempt calibration adjustment or corrective maintenance, which can be adequately performed only by specially trained personnel using specialized equipment. If the operational check of a calibrated instrument is satisfactory, a monitor *must* rely on the instrument reading and *accept* it as an accurate measurement of the gamma dose or dose rate.

2.21 *Environmental Effects.*—Monitoring instruments are manufactured to operate satisfactorily under normally encountered environmental conditions of pressure, temperature and humidity.

2.22 *Response Time.*—Survey meters do not respond instantaneously to changes in dose rate or to changes in the range position. A period of at least fifteen seconds should be allowed for meter response before readings are observed. Dosimeters respond instantaneously to changes in the accumulated dose. During any emergency operation, a monitor should accept the reading on his dosimeter as a measurement of his exposure dose.

2.23 *Care.*—The monitor should prevent radiological contamination of the instruments at all times. Instruments can be placed in a plastic bag to prevent contamination. This is desirable, but not mandatory. In case an instrument becomes contaminated, it can be cleaned with a cloth dampened in a mild soap solution. After decontamination, each instrument should be monitored with a CD V–700, to assure that contaminating material is removed.

2.24 *Limited Standard Items.*—Several radiological instruments are no longer being procured by OCD. These instruments, which have slightly different operating characteristics, ranges, or detection capabilities, are not obsolete instruments and should be used by civil defense organizations possessing them. The CD V–710, 0–50 r/hr gamma survey meter, and the CD V–720, 0–500 r/hr beta-gamma survey meter, are limited standard items. The CD V–715 has superseded these two instruments and is the standard civil defense high range gamma survey meter. However, the CD V–710 and CD V–720, together provide the same gamma capability and have almost identical operating characteristics as the CD V–715. The CD V–730, 0–20r dosimeter, and the CD V–740, 0–100r dosimeter, are also limited standard instruments and have been superseded by the CD V–742. The CD V–710, CD V–720, CD V–730, and CD V–740 should be used for measuring radiation dose or dose rates where they have been issued as components of the radiological monitoring kits.

III. PROTECTIVE MEASURES

3.1 Radiation protection measures are based on the assumption that all radiation exposure is harmful. However, experience and research have shown that if exposure is kept below a certain level, medical care will not be required for the majority of the people. Therefore, adequate methods and procedures for limiting radiation exposure and contamination must be established.

Radiation Hazards

3.2 Radiation is emitted from some fallout particles. The air through which fallout passes and the surfaces on which it settles do not themselves become radioactive. It is the radiation originating from these particles that constitutes the hazard to living things. Of the three types of radiation associated with fallout material, gamma is considered to be the most hazardous. Alpha and beta radiation are relatively easy to shield against, while gamma can require considerable amounts of dense materials or distance between persons and its source in order to prevent radiation damage.

3.3 The major protective measure to be taken by monitors against fallout radiation in the early post-attack period is shelter. In addition, other protective measures such as control of radiation exposure, control of the contamination, and decontamination may be employed from the time of fallout arrival until the radiation hazard no longer restricts living conditions.

Individual Protection

3.4 If the presence of fallout is suspected before the monitor can reach his assigned shelter, the following actions will help minimize its effects:

a. Cover the head with a hat, or a piece of cloth or newspaper.

b. Keep all outer clothing buttoned or zipped. Adjust clothing to cover as much exposed skin as possible.

c. Brush outer clothing periodically.

d. Continue to destination as rapidly as practicable.

3.5 Assume all persons arriving at a shelter or a fallout monitoring station after fallout arrival, and all individuals who have performed outside missions are contaminated. All persons should follow the protective measures outlined in this paragraph.

a. Brush shoes, and shake or brush clothing to remove contamination. This should be done before entering the shelter area.

b. Go to the preselected location in the shelter as described in paragraph 4.8d.

c. Use the CD V-700, with probe shield open, to monitor the clothing after brushing and shaking to determine if further decontamination is necessary. See paragraph 4.8 for details of personnel monitoring.

d. Remove and store all outer clothing in an isolated location if contamination levels after brushing and shaking are too high to be measured with the CD V-700.

e. Wash, brush, or wipe thoroughly, contaminated portions of the skin and hair, being careful not to injure the skin.

f. Monitor the contaminated portions of skin and hair to determine the need for further decontamination. Decontaminate until the CD V-700 indication is approximately equal to the background reading in the shelter.

Collective Protection

3.6 During fallout deposition, all windows, doors, and nonvital vents in sheltered locations should be closed to control the contamination entering the shelter. Similar protective measures should be applied to vehicles.

3.7 When radiation levels become measurable inside the shelter, make a survey of all shelter areas to determine the best protected locations. Repeat this procedure periodically. This information is used to limit the exposure of shelter occupants.

Tasks Outside of Shelter

3.8 When personnel leave shelter, appropriate protective measures should be taken to prevent the contamination of their bodies. Clothing will not protect personnel from gamma but will prevent most air-borne contamination from depositing on the skin, and reduce the need for extensive washing or scrubbing of the body for prevention of beta burns. Most clothing is satisfactory, however, loosely woven clothing should be avoided. Instruct shelter occupants to:

a. Keep time outside of shelter to a minimum when dose rates are high.

b. Wear adequate clothing and cover as much of the body as practicable. Wear boots or rubber galoshes, if available. Tie pant cuffs over them to avoid possible contamination of feet and ankles.

c. Avoid highly contaminated areas whenever possible. Puddles and very dusty areas where contamination is more probable should also be avoided.

d. Under dry and dusty conditions, do not stir up dust unnecessarily. If dusty conditions prevail, a folded man's handkerchief or a folded piece of closely woven cloth should be worn over the nose and mouth to keep the inhalation of fallout to a minimum.

e. Avoid unnecessary contact with contaminated surfaces such as buildings and shrubbery.

3.9 Monitors using vehicles for outside monitoring operations should remain in the vehicle, leaving it only when necessary. To prevent contamination of the interior of the vehicle, all windows and outside vents should be closed when dusty conditions prevail. Vehicles provide only slight protection from gamma but they provide excellent protection from beta and prevent contamination of the occupants.

Food and Water

3.10 To the extent practicable, prevent fallout from becoming mixed into food and water. Food and water which is exposed to radiation, but not contaminated, is not harmed and is fit for.human consumption. If it is suspected that food containers are contaminated, they should be washed or brushed prior to removal of the contents. Food properly removed from such containers will be safe for consumption.

3.11 Water in covered containers and underground sources will be safe. Before the arrival of fallout, open supplies of water such as cisterns, open wells, or other containers should be covered. Shut off the source of supply of potentially contaminated water. All food and water suspected of contamination should be monitored in accordance with paragraph 4.10.

Equipment

3.12 Vehicles and equipment that are required for post-attack operations should be protected from fallout contamination. When practical, all such equipment should be kept under cover in garages and warehouses, or under covers of fabric or plastic. Windows and doors of vehicles and storage areas should be closed.

Control of Exposure

3.13 Monitors are responsible for limiting their exposure and maintaining their personal radiation exposure records. (See attachment A). Radiation exposures of monitoring personnel are likely to lack a uniform pattern. After a period of low exposure, an operational mission may require a high exposure. This may be followed by several days of relatively low exposure before the situation requires an additional heavy exposure. The only reliable method for keeping track of variable exposures is through the use of personal dosimeters and the keeping of complete exposure records.

3.14 All but the most important survival operations should be postponed as long as practicable to take advantage of the decay of fallout. In carrying out high priority tasks exposures should, where practicable, be more or less evenly distributed among operations personnel. Guidance for limiting exposure will be furnished the monitor by the radiological defense officer or other technically qualified civil defense personnel.

IV. MONITORING TECHNIQUES

4.1 This section describes the detailed techniques and procedures for conducting each type of radiological monitoring activity. Fallout station monitors are responsible for performing all of the monitoring techniques outlined in this section. Shelter monitors are responsible for performing all of the techniques except for "Unsheltered Dose Rate Measurements" and "Unsheltered Dose Measurements."

Shelter Area Monitoring

4.2 Dose rates should be measured inside of a shelter or a fallout monitoring station to determine the best shielded portions of the shelter and its immediate adjoining areas. Procedures for this monitoring are:

a. Use the CD V-715.

b. Check the operability of the instrument.

c. Hold the instrument at belt height (3 feet above the ground).

d. Take readings at selected locations throughout the shelter and adjoining areas and record these on a sketch of the area.

Unsheltered Dose Rate Measurements

4.3 Fallout monitoring stations report unsheltered dose rate readings. Procedures for observing unsheltered dose rates are:

a. Use the CD V-715.

b. Check the operability of the instrument.

c. Take a dose rate reading at a specific location in the fallout monitoring station. This should be done as soon as the dose rate reaches or exceeds 0.05 r/hr.

d. Go outside immediately to a preplanned location in a clear, flat area (preferably unpaved), at least 25 feet away from buildings, and take an outside reading. The outside reading should be taken within three minutes of the reading in c. above.

e. Calculate the protection factor of the fallout monitoring station by dividing the outside dose rate by the inside dose rate. The protection factor may vary from location to location within the station. The protection factor referred to here is appropriate only for the location where the inside dose rate measurement is observed.

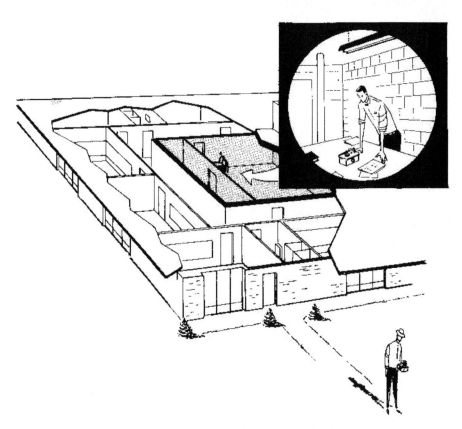

ILLUSTRATION 4.3—Taking readings with the CD V-715.

f. Multiply future inside dose rate readings by the protection factor at the selected location to obtain the outside dose rate. For example: If the inside reading is 0.5 r/hr and the outside reading is 80 r/hr, the *protection factor* can be found by dividing the outside reading by the inside reading. Thus, $80 \div 0.5 =$ a protection factor of 160. If a later inside reading at the same location in the fallout monitoring station is 4 r/hr, the outside dose rate can be calculated by multiplying the protection factor by the inside reading. Thus, $160 \times 4 = 640$ r/hr.

g. Recalculate the protection factor at least once every 24 hours during the first few days postattack, unless the outside dose rate is estimated to be above 100 r/hr. This is necessary because the energy of gamma radiation is changing, thus changing the protection factor of the fallout monitoring station.

h. Record and report the dose rate measurement in accordance with the organization SOP.

i. Take all dose rate measurements outside after the unsheltered dose rate has decreased to 25 r/hr.

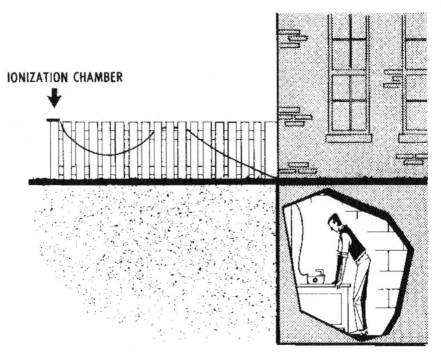

IONIZATION CHAMBER

ILLUSTRATION 4.4—Taking reading with the CD V 717.

4.4 When the CD V–717 remote reading instrument is available, it may be used for taking outside dose rate measurements. The CD V–717 could be used as follows:

a. Position the instrument at a selected location within the fallout monitoring station.

b. Place the removable ionization chamber 3 feet above the ground in a reasonably flat area and at least 20 feet from the fallout station. Preferably this should be done prior to fallout arrival. It is desirable to cover the ionization chamber with a light plastic bag or other lightweight material.

c. Observe outside dose rates directly.

d. Record and report dose rates in accordance with the organization SOP.

Unsheltered Dose Measurements

4.5 Fallout monitoring stations report unsheltered dose readings. Procedures for taking these readings are:

a. Zero a CD V–742.

b. Measure the unsheltered dose rate in accordance with paragraph 4.3.

16

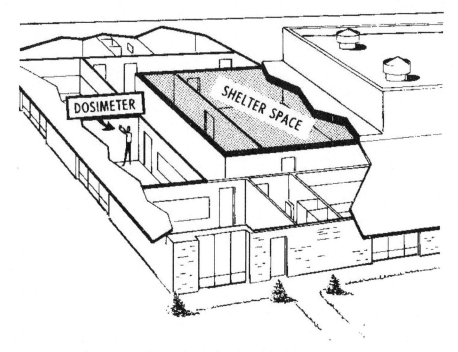

ILLUSTRATION 4.5—Unsheltered dose reading with the CD V–742.

c. Select an inside location where the dose rate is approximately one-tenth to one-twentieth of the unsheltered dose rate and position the CD V 742 at this location.

d. Determine the protection factor for this location in accordance with paragraph 4.3 c–e.

e. Read the CD V–742 daily. If the daily dose at this location could exceed 200r, estimate the time required for a 150r exposure on the CD V 742. Record this reading, rezero the dosimeter, and reposition it. To determine the daily unsheltered dose, multiply the daily dose at this location by the protection factor.

f. Record the readings and rezero the instrument.

Personnel Dose Measurements

4.6 The monitor must determine the daily exposure dose of all shelterees or fallout monitoring station occupants. Procedures for determining daily doses are:

a. Zero all available CD V 742's.

b. Position the dosimeters so that representative shelter exposures will be measured by the instruments. The monitor must exercise judgment in positioning these instruments. The protection factor may vary considerably at different locations within the shelter. The instruments

17

should be placed within the areas of greatest occupancy, which may change with time. During the early high radiation period, occupancy will be concentrated in the high protection areas of the shelter. Later, the occupancy of the shelter can be expanded. If representative readings are to be obtained, the dosimeters must follow the location shifts of the occupants.

c. If several dosimeters are positioned in one compartment, read the dosimeters each day and average the total doses. Recharge dosimeters which read more than half scale. If some shelters are divided into compartments or rooms that may have different protection factors, the dose should be measured or calculated for each compartment.

d. Instruct the shelter occupants to record their individual doses on their radiation exposure record (See attachment A), as approved by the shelter manager. Exposure entries should be made to the nearest roentgen. If there is no measurable dose, continue to read the dosimeters each day. Record an accumulated dose for a few days' period, if measurable.

4.7 If monitors or other persons are required to go outside, these additional exposures should be measured and the doses recorded.

Personnel Monitoring

4.8 Procedures for personnel monitoring are:

a. Use the CD V–700. Attach the headphone because this allows the monitor to visually follow and better control the position of the probe while monitoring. The headphone also responds more quickly to changes in radiation levels than the meter.

b. Check the operability of the instrument.

c. Place the probe in a light plastic bag or cover of light-weight material to prevent contamination. This is desirable, but not mandatory.

d. Select a reception location for conducting the monitoring operation. Precautions should be taken to prevent contamination of the shelter area. If possible, a reception area for monitoring personnel should be located in a room adjoining the shelter area. If this is not possible, an in-shelter area near the entrance should be selected and restricted to this purpose.

e. Determine the background radiation level periodically at the location where the monitoring is to take place. If the meter indication is above 50 mr/hr with the probe shield open, find a better shielded location that will bring the meter indication below 30 mr/hr. This might be done by selecting a different location in the shelter and/or sweeping the area several times to reduce possible contamination. If this fails, the shielding can be improved by stacking shelter supplies and other materials around the individual to be monitored.

f. Open the shield on the CD V–700 probe and put on the headphone.

g. Place the probe about two inches from the person's body being careful not to touch him. Starting at the top of the head, move the probe

18

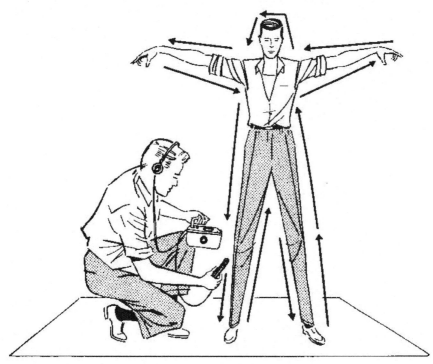

ILLUSTRATION 4.8—Personnel Monitoring.

downward on one side of the neck, collar, shoulder, arm, wrist, hand, underarm, armpit, side, leg, cuff, and shoe. Monitor the insides of the legs and the other side of the body in the sequence indicated in illustration 4.8. Monitor the front and back of the body. Pay particular attention to the feet, seat, elbows, armpits, and hairy or moist areas.

h. Decontaminate shelter occupants found to be contaminated as described in paragraph 3.5.

i. Monitor individuals after decontamination to determine that contamination has been effectively removed. Repeat decontamination procedures if required.

Food and Water Monitoring

4.9 Food and water monitoring criteria and techniques are being reevaluated and are subject to change.

4.10 Potentially contaminated supplies of food and water should be monitored to determine if they are acceptable for human consumption. A procedure for monitoring food or water follows:

a. Use the CD V-700.

b. Check the operability of the instrument.

c. Select an area that is shielded or can be shielded so that the meter indication is as low as possible. Since the space required to conduct this

19

type of monitoring will be small, it should not be difficult to improvise a shielded area, if needed. Determine the background radiation.

d. Monitor the food or water at a distance of approximately one inch from its surface, with the probe shield open.

e. Observe the meter indication. If it increases above background, contamination is present.

4.11 Do not discard contaminated food or water. It should be decontaminated and rechecked, or placed in storage and rechecked at a later date for possible consumption after the contamination has decreased due to radioactive decay. Foods such as fruits and vegetables could be decontaminated by washing, brushing or peeling. Water which is heavily contaminated might be improved by filtering, or by allowing any particles to settle out. If only contaminated food or water is available, the monitor should determine which portions are *least* contaminated. If its use becomes necessary, the monitor should recommend that supplies with the smallest amount of contamination should be used first.

Area Monitoring

4.12 Area monitoring is used to locate zones of contamination and determine the dose rates within these zones. The monitor should be informed by his radiological defense officer concerning routes to be followed, locations where readings are needed, the mission dose, and the estimated time needed to accomplish the mission.

a. Plan to keep personal exposure doses as low as possible.
   (1) Know the specific accomplishment, extent, and importance of each monitoring mission.
   (2) Know the allowable exposure dose for each mission and the expected dose rates to be encountered.
   (3) Make allowances for the exposure to be received traveling to and from the monitoring area. Obtain information about the condition of roads, bridges, etc., that might interfere with the mission and lengthen exposure time.

b. Clothing needed for the mission.
   (1) Tie pant cuffs over boots or leggings.
   (2) Wear a protective mask, gloves, head covering, and sufficient clothing to cover skin areas when dusty conditions prevail. If no masks are available, cover the nose and mouth with a handkerchief.

c. Equipment needed for the mission.
   (1) Use the CD V-715. If the dose rates are expected to be below 50 mr/hr, also carry the CD V-700.
   (2) Wear a CD V-742.
   (3) Carry contamination signs, if areas are to be marked. This may also require stakes, heavy cord, hammer, and nails for posting the signs.
   (4) Carry a pencil, paper, and a map with monitoring points marked.

d. Procedures for area monitoring are:
   (1) Zero the dosimeter before leaving the shelter and place it in a pocket to protect it from possible contamination.
   (2) Check the operability of the CD V-715 and CD V-700, if it is to be used.
   (3) Use vehicles such as autos, trucks, bicycles, or motorcycles when distances are too great to cover quickly on foot. Keep auto and truck cab windows and vents closed when traveling under extremely dusty conditions. The use of a bicycle or motorcycle may be more practical if roadways are blocked.
   (4) Take readings at about three feet (belt high) above the ground. If readings are taken from a moving vehicle, the instrument should be positioned on the seat beside the driver. If readings are to be taken outside a vehicle, the monitor should move several feet away from the vehicle to take the reading.
   (5) Record the dose rate, the time and location for each reading. If readings are taken within a vehicle, this should be noted in the report.
   (6) Post markers, if required by the mission. The marker should face away from the restricted area. Write the date, time, and dose rate on the back of the marker.
   (7) Read the pocket dosimeter at frequent intervals to determine when return to shelter should begin. Allowances should be made for the dose to be received during return to the shelter.
   (8) Remove outer clothing on return to the shelter and check all personnel for contamination.
   (9) Decontaminate, if required.
   (10) Report results of the survey.
   (11) Record radiation exposure.

Dose Rate Readings From Dosimeters

4.13 Survey instruments should always be used to measure dose rates. However, if no operable survey instruments are available, dosimeters can be used to calculate dose rates as follows:

a. Zero a CD V-742.

b. Place the zeroed dosimeter at a selected location.

c. Expose the dosimeter for a measured interval of time, but do not remain in the radiation field while the dosimeter is being exposed. This interval should be sufficient to allow the dosimeter to read at least 10r. It may take one or two trials before the proper interval can be selected.

d. Read the dosimeter.

e. Divide sixty minutes by the number of minutes the dosimeter was exposed. Multiply this number by the measured dose. Example: If the dose is 10r for a measured interval of five minutes, the dose rate can be calculated as follows:

$$(60 \div 5) \times 10 = 12 \times 10 = 120 \text{ r/hr.}$$

V. MONITORING OPERATIONS

5.1 Radiological monitors, whether assigned to shelters or fallout monitoring stations, perform essentially similar operations. Any departures from the operations described in this section will be the result of decisions by the State and local civil defense organizations and must be reflected in their SOP's. If local or State SOP's are not in existence, monitors should follow the procedures outlined in this section.

Readiness Operations

5.2 During peacetime, all assigned monitors will:

a. Perform an operational check on all survey meters and rezero all dosimeters every two months.

b. Record the results on the Inspection, Maintenance, and Calibration Log. (See attachment B.)

c. Initiate action for the repair or replacement of inoperable instruments according to the organizational SOP.

d. Replace batteries annually or sooner if necessary.

e. Make instruments available for calibration as required by the organizational SOP.

f. Participate in refresher training exercises and tests as required.

g. Prepare copies of a sketch of the assigned shelter and adjoining areas for use during shelter occupancy.

h. Plan a location in the shelter, in coordination with the shelter manager, to serve as the center of monitoring operations.

Shelter Operations

5.3 Upon attack or warning of attack, a shelter monitor reports to the shelter manager in his assigned shelter and performs the following *check list* of operations in order:

a. Perform an operational check on all survey meters.

b. Charge dosimeters.

c. Position dosimeters at predesignated locations in the shelter.

d. Report to the shelter manager on the condition of the instruments and the positioning of dosimeters.

e. Check to see that doors, windows, or other openings are closed during fallout deposition.

f. Begin outside surface monitoring to determine the time of fallout arrival. Advise the shelter manager when the dose rate begins to increase.

g. Monitor all personnel entering shelter after fallout starts to determine if they are contaminated. Personnel monitoring may be impracticable in some shelters because (1) radiation levels or contamination levels inside the shelter may be too high, or (2) the influx of persons into the shelter may be too large to permit the monitoring of each person. In the event of high radiation or contamination levels, delay monitoring until it can be performed in accordance with procedures outlined in paragraph 4.8. In the event of a large influx of persons into the shelter, monitor several persons selected at random to determine the extent of personal contamination. If practical, segregate groups suspected of heavy contamination until each individual can be monitored.

h. Insure that all persons who have performed outside missions in contaminated areas, follow the protective actions outlined in paragraph 3.5.

i. Monitor all food, water, and equipment brought to a shelter after fallout arrival to determine if they are safe to use. Food and water stored in the shelter should be acceptable for consumption. Leave contaminated items outside the shelter or place them in isolated storage near the shelter.

j. Take readings at selected locations throughout the shelter and record the dose rates on prepared sketches of the area. Particular attention should be given to monitoring any occupied areas close to filters in the ventilating system. Show the time of readings on all sketches.

k. Furnish all sketches to the shelter manager and recommend one of the following courses of action:
   (1) Occupy only those areas with dose rates below 2 r/hr.
   (2) If dose rates are not uniform and above 2 r/hr throughout the shelter, occupy the areas with lowest dose rates.
   (3) If space prohibits locating all shelter occupants in the better protected areas, rotate personnel to distribute exposure evenly. Do not rotate personnel unless there is a difference of 10r in the exposure between the best and the least protected shelter occupants. Under all conditions, give consideration to providing the best available protection to pregnant women, children under 18 years, and personnel assigned to early emergency operations.

l. Repeat the procedures in paragraph j at least once daily. If there is a rapid change in the dose rate, repeat at least once every six hours.

m. Inform the shelter manager to notify the appropriate control center and request guidance if: (1) at any time during the shelter period the inside dose rate reaches or exceeds 10 r/hr, or (2) within any two days period of shelter the dose is 75r.

n. Issue each shelter occupant a Radiation Exposure Record. As approved by the shelter manager, advise each person once daily of their exposure during the previous 24 hours. Follow procedures in paragraph 4.6 to calculate the exposure of shelter occupants.

5.4 During the latter part of the shelter period, when there is less frequent need for in-shelter monitoring, some of the shelter monitors may be required to provide monitoring services in support of other civil defense operations. A monitoring capability should always be retained in the shelter until the end of the shelter period.

5.5 At the conclusion of the shelter period, all shelter monitors, except those regularly assigned to emergency services, may expect reassignment.

Monitoring Fallout Station Operations

5.6 For his own protection and the protection of all members of a fallout monitoring station, the monitor should perform the same shelter operations as described in paragraph 5.3. *In addition*, the fallout station monitor will measure, record, and report unsheltered dose and dose rates to the appropriate control center. Unless otherwise specified by the local SOP, the monitor will:

a. Make a FLASH REPORT when the outside dose rate reaches or exceeds 0.5 r/hr. The report will be in the following form:

tttt   eeeFallout

where,
tttt is the time of the fallout observation in local time and eee is the identifier for the monitoring station.

b. Record and report dose and dose rates in accordance with the Radiological Reporting Log. (See Attachment C.)

c. Record and report dose rates as follows:

tttt   eeerrr

where,
tttt is the time of the reading in local time; eee is the station designator; and rrr is the measured dose rate. Using the Time Conversion Chart on the reverse side of the Radiological Reporting Log, enter above each "Z" time designation the corresponding time for your locality. "Z" time is a common reference time essential to analysis and evaluation of radiological data by radiological defense officers and is often referred to as Greenwich Meridian Time. It is important that the monitor convert and record these times in the appropriate spaces on his log to assure that all reports have a common reference time.

Dose rates will be reported in roentgens per hour (r/hr) as a three digit number. Example: For readings of less than 100, the first digit will be zero. A reading of 75 r/hr will be reported as 075. If the reading is less than 10 r/hr, then there will be two zeros followed by the reading. Thus, a reading of 5 r/hr will be reported as 005. Dose rates which equal or exceed 1 r/hr will be reported to the nearest whole r/hr. Thus, 1.4 r/hr will be reported as 001, and 1.5 r/hr will be reported as 002. When dose rates that have exceeded 1 r/hr have decreased to less than 1 r/hr, they will be expressed in tenths, hundredths, or thousandths of r/hr as required. Thus, 1/10 r/hr will be reported as .100, 50 mr/hr will be reported as .050. The number or letter designation of the fallout station will be assigned by the CD organization and should always be reported exactly as assigned.

d. Record and report dose measurements as follows:

dose eeerrrr

where,

eee is the station designator and rrrr is the total dose in roentgens to date.

Monitoring in Support of Emergency Operations

5.7 As soon as radiation levels decrease sufficiently to permit high priority operations and later, as operational recovery activities including decontamination of vital areas and structures are begun, all fallout station monitors and most shelter monitors are required to provide radiological monitoring support to these operations. Radiological defense officers will direct the systematic monitoring of areas, routes, equipment and facilities to determine the extent of contamination. This information will help the civil defense organization determine when people may leave shelter, what areas may be occupied, what routes may be used, and what areas and facilities must be decontaminated.

5.8 Many emergency services personnel, such as fire, police, health, and welfare personnel, will serve as shelter monitors or fallout station monitors during the shelter period. However, as operational recovery activities are begun, they will have primary responsibility in their own fields, with secondary responsibilities in radiological defense. Most services will provide for a radiological monitoring capability for the protection of their operational crews performing emergency activities. The capability is provided until the radiological defense officer determines that it is not required. Services provide this capability from their own ranks, to the extent practical, supported by shelter monitors and fallout station monitors, when required.

5.9 When a service is directed to perform a mission, the control center furnishes the following information:

a. The time when the service may leave shelter to perform its mission.

b. The allowable dose for the complete mission; that is, from time of departure until return to shelter.

c. The dose rate to be expected in the area of the mission.

5.10 The monitor supporting emergency operations will:

a. Read his instruments frequently during each operation and advise the individual in charge of the mission on necessary radiological protective measures and when the crew should leave the area and return to shelter to avoid exceeding the planned mission dose.

b. Determine the effectiveness of decontamination measures, if supporting decontamination operations.

c. Monitor all personnel and equipment on return to shelter, or base of operations, to determine if they are contaminated.

d. Direct decontamination of personnel and equipment, if necessary, and assure that decontamination procedures have been effective.

VI. GUIDANCE FOR INDEPENDENT OPERATIONS

6.1 All monitors receive technical direction and guidance from the RADEF officer or other qualified civil defense personnel. However, under the conditions of nuclear attack, communications with the control center could be disrupted. At any time during the shelter period that communications with the assigned control center are disrupted, an effort should be made to contact a neighboring shelter or fallout monitoring station through which RADEF advice and guidance could be relayed. If this effort is unsuccessful, the monitor may, after consultation with the shelter manager or individual in charge of the fallout monitoring station, use the following guidance **As a Last Resort**. The guidance equips the monitor with a means of making very rough approximations on which to take critical actions.

Permissible Activities

6.2 When the dose rates inside and outside of the shelter or fallout monitoring station are known, use the following as a guide for permissible activities. This guidance is based on observations made on large groups of people and, therefore, should be used with caution with small groups of individuals. Again, it is furnished only as a **Last Resort Guide**. The data must be modified as early as possible, taking into account the age of the fallout. If the fallout is relatively young (2 or 3 hours old) greater relaxation of shelter control can be tolerated than that indicated below. Conversely, if the fallout is relatively old (several days or weeks), more rigid control would be required. If in-shelter doses exceed 75r, activities should, if possible, be restricted even more than indicated below.

TABLE 6.2

If the outside dose rate has fallen to: (in r/hr)	Permissible Activities
Less than 0.5	No special precautions are necessary for operational activities. Keep fallout from contaminating people. Sleep in the shelter.
0.5 to 2	Outdoor activity (up to a few hours per day) is acceptable for essential purposes such as: fire fighting, police action, rescue, repair, securing necessary food, water, medicine and blankets, important communication, disposal of waste, exercise and obtaining fresh air. Eat, sleep, and carry on all other activities in the best available shelter.

If the outside dose rate has fallen to: (in r/hr)	Permissible Activities
2 to 10	Periods of less than an hour per day of outdoor activity are acceptable for the most essential purposes. Shelter occupants should rotate outdoor tasks to distribute exposures. Outdoor activities of children should be limited to 10 to 15 minutes per day. Activities such as repair or exercise may take place in less than optimum shelter.
10 to 100	Time outside of the shelter should be held to a few minutes and limited to those few activities that cannot be postponed. All people should remain in the best available shelter no matter how uncomfortable.
Greater than 100	Outdoor activity of more than a few minutes may result in sickness or death. Occasions which might call for outside activity are: (1) risk of death or serious injury in present shelter from fire, collapse, thirst, etc., and (2) present shelter is greatly inadequate—might result in fatality—and better shelter is known to be only a few minutes away.

6.3 If communications are disrupted, the monitors at the fallout monitoring stations will continue to record the information required in paragraph 5.6 and report the information to a control center as soon as communications are restored.

Symptoms of Radiation Injury

6.4 Radiation from fallout causes injury to body tissue. Over a period of time the body is able to repair most of this injury, provided the individual survives. Observable symptoms of radiation sickness are: nausea, vomiting, diarrhea, fever, listlessness, and a general feeling of fatigue. Some or all of these symptoms may appear within the first three days. They may then disappear, reappearing after a week or so, sometimes accompanied by bloody diarrhea and swelling of the nasal passages, mouth and throat. Generally speaking, the greater the dose, the earlier the symptoms will appear. They will be more severe and last longer.

6.5 Beta burns will result from significant amounts of fallout remaining in direct contact with the skin. Early symptoms include itching and burning sensations which may soon disappear. After two weeks or more, there may be a loss of hair, which will return in about 6 months. Development of darkened or raised skin areas or sores appears within one or two weeks depending on the severity of the burn. The harmful effects of fallout taken into the body may be long delayed and are not readily recognized.

6.6 The severity of effects on individuals exposed to the same dose will vary widely. However, Table 6.6 may be used to estimate short-term effects on humans of external gamma exposures of less than four days.

28

TABLE 6.6

Short-term dose	Visible effect
50r	No visible effects.
75–100r	Brief periods of nausea on day of exposure in about 10% of the group.
200r	As many as 50% of this group may experience some of the symptoms of radiation sickness. Although only 5% to 10% may require medical attention, no deaths are expected.
450r	Serious radiation sickness in most members of the group followed by death to about 50% within two to four weeks.
600r	Serious radiation sickness in all members of the group followed by death to almost all members within one to three weeks.

Care of Radiation Casualties

6.7 If a person becomes ill from exposure to radiation, he should be placed under the care of a physician or medical technician, if possible. In the post-attack situation, medical care may be very limited. Care consists primarily of keeping the patient comfortable and in bed. Keep the patient clean and isolated from infectious diseases. The ill person should have liquids to replace the body fluids lost as a result of vomiting and diarrhea as soon as he can tolerate them. Nourishing foods should be given the patient since they are needed for recovery.

6.8 Beta burns are treated in the same manner as burns resulting from heat. If possible, allow a physician or medical technician to treat the beta burns.

Exposure Criteria

6.9 Keep the exposure of shelterees as low as practicable. With a good shelter in most fallout areas, it should be possible to keep exposure doses below 100r during the first 2 weeks. Keep the total exposure of personnel on emergency missions below 200r during the first month of operations. Keep additional exposures to less than 25r/week for the next 5 months.

Dose and Dose Rate Calculations

6.10 Nomograms, based on theoretical fallout radiation decay characteristics, may be used for rough estimates of future dose rates and radiation doses that might be expected in performing necessary tasks outside the shelter. However, when fallout from several nuclear weapons detonated more than 24 hours apart is deposited in an area, the decay rate may differ markedly from the assumed decay rate. For this reason, calculations using nomograms should be limited as follows:

a. The time of detonation must be known with a reasonable degree of accuracy plus or minus one hour for forecasts made within the first twelve hours, and plus or minus 2–3 hours for later forecasts.

b. If nuclear detonations occur more than 24 hours apart, predicted dose rates may be considerably in error. In this case, use the H hour of the latest detonation to compute "Time After Burst."

c. At the time of calculation, dose rates must have been decreasing for at least 2–3 hours, and forecasts should be made for periods no further in the future than the length of time the radiation levels have been observed to decrease.

6.11 For unsheltered emergency missions, the effects of the mission exposure must be weighed against the benefit to be derived and the importance of early mission performance. The longer the task can be delayed without undue penalty, the greater the radioactive decay of the fallout and the less the radiation penalty. Generally, outside missions should be short, not to exceed three hours. *Missions will not be started until monitoring indicates that predicted conditions actually prevail.* At least one dosimeter will be carried and periodically read to assure limiting the dose to the established value.

6.12 To use the **Dose Rate Nomogram** (See attachment D) connect a known dose rate in the "Dose Rate at H+t" column with the corresponding time in the "Time After Burst" column. Note the reading on the "Dose Rate at H+1" column. Connect this reading with the time of the unknown dose rate on the "Time After Burst" column and read the answer from the "Dose Rate at H+t" column.

Example:

Given—The dose rate in an area at H+12 is 50 r/hr.

Find—The dose rate in this area at H+18.

Solution:

Using a straightedge, connect 50 r/hr on the "Dose Rate at H+t" column with 12 hours on the "Time After Burst" column and read 970 r/hr on the "Dose Rate at H+1" column. Pivot the straightedge to connect 970 r/hr on the "Dose Rate at H+1" column with 18 hours on the "Time After Burst" column and read the answer from the "Dose Rate at H+t" column.

Answer—31 r/hr

6.13 To use the "Entry Time—Stay Time—Total Dose Nomograms" (See Attachment E), connect two known quantities with a straightedge and locate the point on the "D/R₁" column where the straightedge crosses it. Connect this point with a third known quantity and read the answer from the appropriate column.

a. Example (Total Dose):

Given—The dose rate in an area at H+8 is 10 r/hr.

Find—The total dose received if a person enters this area at H+10 and remains for four hours.

Solution:

Find the dose rate at H+1 (120 r/hr) as described in paragraph 6.12. Using a straightedge, connect four hours on the "Stay Time" column with ten hours on the "Entry Time" column. Find .21 on the "D/R₁" column. Connect .21 on the "D/R₁" column with 120 r/hr on the "Dose Rate at H+1" column. Read the answer from the "Total Dose" column.

Answer—25r

b. Example (Entry Time):

Given—Dose rate in an area at H+10 is 12 r/hr. Stay time is 8 hours and the mission dose is established at 50r.

Find—The earliest entry time into the area.

Solution:

Find the dose rate at H+1 (190 r/hr) as described in paragraph 6.12. Using a straightedge, connect 50r on the "Total Dose" column with 190 r/hr on the "Dose Rate at H+1" column. Find .26 on the "D/R₁" column. Connect .26 on the "D/R₁" column with 3 hours on the "Stay Time" column. Read the answer from the "Entry Time" column.

Answer—14 hours

...

ATTACHMENT A

RADIATION EXPOSURE RECORD				Date(s) of Exposure(s)	Daily Dose(s)	Total Dose to Date
Name JOHN DOE						
Address 227 N. Moorland						
Battle Creek, Michigan						
Soc. Sec. No. 545-26-5535						

Date(s) of Exposure(s)	Daily Dose(s)	Total Dose to Date
6/6/62	15	15
6/7/62	5	20
6/7/62	25	45
6/8-10/62	5	50
DATE		

FRONT SIDE   **SAMPLE FORM**   **BACK SIDE**

Example:

From the illustration shown above on June 6 the individual received a sheltered dose of 15r, and on June 7 he received a sheltered dose of 5r and an additional outside dose of 25r. The two June 7 exposures have been recorded as two entries. On June 8 and 9 the dosimeter reading inside the shelter was so low it could not be read. On June 10, a reading of 5r was measurable. In order to account for the 3 days, a 5r entry was made on June 10.

ATTACHMENT B

INSPECTION, MAINTENANCE AND CALIBRATION LOG FOR RADIOLOGICAL INSTRUMENTS

DATE	ACTION	REMARKS	SIGNATURE
8/1/62	inspection	O.K.	JOHN DOE
10/3/62	inspection	O.K. except CD V-715	JOHN DOE
	out for repair	CD V-715, #86376	JOHN DOE
10/15/62	returned	CD V-715, #86376	JOHN DOE
12/2/62	inspection	O.K.	JOHN DOE
1/6/63	batteries replaced		JOHN DOE
1/15/63	calibration	O.K.	JOHN DOE

SAMPLE FORM

Directions:

1. Keep this log with the instruments.
2. Inspect all radiological instruments every two months. Perform an operational check on survey meters and, if necessary, rezero all dosimeters. Enter the results of the inspection on this log.
3. Initiate action for repair or replacement of inoperable instruments. Enter the appropriate action on this log.
4. Replace batteries annually or sooner, if necessary. Enter replacement on this log.
5. Make instruments available for calibration as required. Enter action on this log.

34

ATTACHMENT C

STATION _____

RADIOLOGICAL REPORTING LOG   REPORTED TO _____

Flash report (0.5 r/hr. or more) _____

	1st hr. thru 12th hr.[3] (hourly on the hour)		13th hr. thru 24th hr.[3] (every 3 hours)		25th hr. thru 48th hr.[3] (every 6 hours)		After 48th hr.[3] (daily at 0300Z)	
Date _____							Date	Dose rate r/hr	Total dose[2]
Time _____	Dose Rate r/hr		Date Time	Dose Rate r/hr	Date Time	Dose Rate r/hr			
Dose Rate _____ r/hr	1.		1.		1.			_____	_____
Time sent to control center _____	2.		2.		2.			_____	_____
	3.		3.		3.			_____	_____
Note: Flash report of fall-out will be made as soon as dose rate reaches 0.5 r/hr.	4.		4.		4.			_____	_____
	5.		5.		Take observations at			_____	_____
	6.		6.					_____	_____
	7.		7.					_____	_____
	8.		8.		0300Z 0900Z 1500Z 2100Z			_____	_____
Report as follows:	9.		Take observations at		[2] Total dose to 0300Z				
	10.								
1. _____ (Time of observ.)	11.		0300Z 0600Z 0900Z 1200Z		If at any time following a period of decay, the dose rate increases materially, file a special report and start new program of observations.				
	12.		1500Z 1800Z 2100Z 2400Z						
2. _____ (Location)	[2] Total dose to 0300Z		[2] Total dose to 0300Z						
Fallout _____									
3. _____									

Report dose rates as follows:

1. _____ Time _____
2. _____ Location _____
3. _____ Dose Rate _____
4. Dose to _____ 0300Z

[1] Enter local time from reverse side.
[2] Total dose read from dosimeter—Cumulative from arrival of fallout.
[3] After flash report.

35

TIME CONVERSION CHART

Greenwich Mean Time	Eastern Daylight	Eastern Standard or Central Daylight	Central Standard or Mountain Daylight	Mountain Standard or Pacific Daylight	Pacific Standard
0100	2100*	2000*	1900*	1800*	1700*
0200	2200*	2100*	2000*	1900*	1800*
0300	2300*	2200*	2100*	2000*	1900*
0400	2400*	2300*	2200*	2100*	2000*
0500	0100	2400*	2300*	2200*	2100*
0600	0200	0100	2400*	2300*	2200*
0700	0300	0200	0100	2400*	2300*
0800	0400	0300	0200	0100	2400*
0900	0500	0400	0300	0200	0100
1000	0600	0500	0400	0300	0200
1100	0700	0600	0500	0400	0300
1200	0800	0700	0600	0500	0400
1300	0900	0800	0700	0600	0500
1400	1000	0900	0800	0700	0600
1500	1100	1000	0900	0800	0700
1600	1200	1100	1000	0900	0800
1700	1300	1200	1100	1000	0900
1800	1400	1300	1200	1100	1000
1900	1500	1400	1300	1200	1100
2000	1600	1500	1400	1300	1200
2100	1700	1600	1500	1400	1300
2200	1800	1700	1600	1500	1400
2300	1900	1800	1700	1600	1500
2400	2000	1900	1800	1700	1600

*Add 1 day to the local Calendar date for equivalent date in GMT. Example: Observed Central Standard Time is 10:00 PM (2200 CST) on the 14th day of the month (142200 CST). Expressed as GMT, that time would be 0400Z on the 15th day of the month (150400Z).

DOSE RATE

NOMOGRAM

(FOR PLANNING PURPOSES)

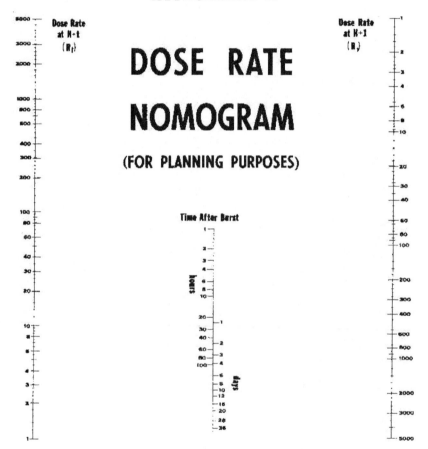

ENTRY TIME - STAY TIME TOTAL DOSE NOMOGRAM

(FOR PLANNING PURPOSES)

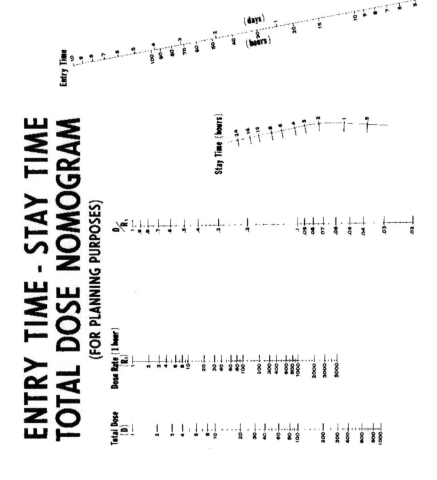

38

GLOSSARY

The following are the meanings of the indicated terms as they are used in this handbook.

Alpha

Particles emitted from the nuclei of heavy radioactive atoms such as radium, uranium, or plutonium. Alpha particles do not penetrate the skin and, thus, are not an external hazard. If emitted inside the body, they can cause severe damage in the tissue very close to the source. It is unlikely that fallout from efficient nuclear explosions will emit significant amounts of alpha radiation.

Beta

Particles emitted from the nuclei of some types of radioactive atoms. When heavy atoms are split in a nuclear detonation the fragments formed are usually beta emitters. Most fallout beta radiation has sufficient penetrating power to cause skin "burns" if a high concentration of fallout particles remains in contact with the skin for several hours. If fission products are taken into the body, beta radiation can be an internal hazard.

Calibration

Determination of variation in accuracy of radiological instruments. Radioactive sources are used to produce known dose rates. The variation in accuracy of a radiological instrument can be determined by measuring these known dose rates.

Contamination

The deposit of radioactive material on the surfaces of structures, areas, objects, or personnel following a nuclear explosion. This generally consists of fallout in which radioactive bomb fragments and other weapon debris have become incorporated with particles of dirt.

Decontamination

The reduction or removal of contaminating radioactive fallout from a structure, area, object, or person. Decontamination may be accomplished by (1) treating the surface so as to remove or decrease the contamination; (2) letting the material stand so that the radioactivity is decreased as a result of natural decay; and (3) covering the contamination so as to attenuate the radiation emitted.

Dose

Accumulated or total exposure to gamma radiation, commonly expressed in roentgens.

Dose Rate

The rate or dose per unit time of exposure to gamma radiation, commonly expressed in roentgens per hour, r/hr, or milliroentgens per hour, mr/hr.

Emergency Services

Elements of government that are responsible for the protection of life and property, such as fire, police, welfare, and rescue services.

Fallout

The process of the fallback to the earth's surface of particles contaminated with radioactive bomb fragments from a nuclear explosion. Most of the fallout from a surface burst will be deposited within 24 hours after a nuclear explosion and within 400 to 500 miles downwind from ground zero.

Fallout Monitoring Station

A designated facility such as a fire station, police or public works building, or other location which should have a protection factor of at least 100 and relatively reliable communications. It may be established with a minimum of two trained radiological monitors but as promptly as feasible the number should be increased to a minimum of four.

Gamma

Nuclear radiation of high energy originating in atomic nuclei and accompanying many beta particles as they are emitted from the fragments of heavy atoms split in a nuclear detonation. Physically, gamma rays are identical with x-rays of high energy. Gamma rays are very penetrating and for practical shielding considerable amounts of dense material is usually employed.

Milliroentgen

1/1000 of a roentgen. 1000 milliroentgens equal one roentgen. See roentgen.

Monitor

An individual trained to: measure, record, and report radiation dose and dose rates; provide limited field guidance on radiation hazards associated with operations to which he is assigned; and perform operator's maintenance of radiological instruments.

Protection Factor

A factor used to express the relation between the amount of fallout gamma radiation that would be received by an unprotected person compared to the amount he would receive if he were in a shelter. For example, an unprotected person would be exposed to 100 times more radiation than a person inside a shelter with a protection factor of 100.

Radiation

Nuclear radiation. Energy and particles emitted from the nuclei of radioactive atoms. The important nuclear radiations from radioactive fallout are beta particles and gamma rays.

Radioactivity

The spontaneous breakdown of nuclei of unstable atoms with the resulting emission of nuclear radiation, generally alpha or beta particles, often accompanied by gamma rays.

Radiological Defense

The organized effort, through detection, warning, and preventative and remedial measures to minimize the effects of nuclear radiation on people and resources.

Readiness Operations

Plans and preparations made during peacetime for survival and recovery operations during and after a nuclear attack.

Remedial Movement

Transfer of people *after* a nuclear attack to provide better fallout protection. This can be accomplished by moving people to a shelter with a higher protection factor or to an area where the dose rates are lower.

Roentgen

A unit of measure for gamma (or x-ray) radiation exposure.

Shelter

A habitable structure or space stocked with essential provisions and used to protect its occupants from fallout radiation.

Shelter Period

The interval of time from attack, or warning of attack, until dose rates from fallout have decreased to a level which will permit people to leave shelter. This time may vary from a few hours to several days or weeks depending upon the degree of the fallout hazard.

Standing Operating Procedures (SOP)

A set of instructions having the force of a directive, covering those features of operations which lend themselves to a definite or standardized procedure without loss of effectiveness.

41

U.S. GOVERNMENT PRINTING OFFICE: 1963   O—680953

facts about

FALLOUT

protection

FIVE STEPS TO SAFETY

LEARN:

1. Warning signals and what they mean.

2. Your community plan for emergency action.

3. Protection from radioactive fallout.

4. First aid and home emergency preparedness.

5. Use of CONELRAD—640 or 1240—for official directions.

For sale by the Superintendent of Documents,
U. S. Government Printing Office,
Washington 25, D. C. — Price 10 cents

**EXECUTIVE OFFICE
OF THE PRESIDENT**

**OFFICE OF CIVIL AND
DEFENSE MOBILIZATION**

April 1958   L–18
[Reprinted September 1958]

* U. S. GOVERNMENT PRINTING OFFICE   1958 O—483193

FALLOUT?

Fallout is tiny pieces of dust and debris, which are made radioactive by nuclear explosions. When a hydrogen bomb is exploded close to the ground, thousands of tons of these tiny particles of dust and debris are sucked upward high into the air. They help form the mushroom cloud which is always seen with one of these explosions.

Some of this radioactive matter spills out of the cloud near the explosion. Most of it is carried by the wind for many miles. Eventually it settles to earth. It is called fallout and continues to give off radioactivity until it decays.

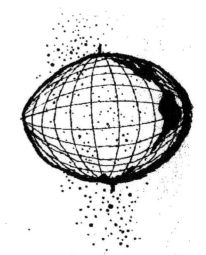

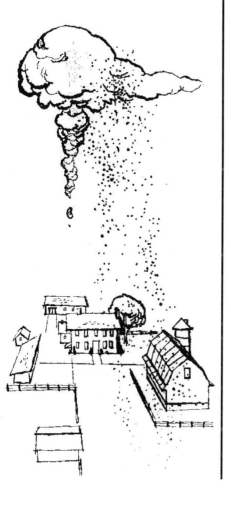

RADIOACTIVITY IS NOTHING NEW

THE WHOLE WORLD IS RADIOACTIVE

But normal amounts of it are not dangerous. Only when radioactivity is present in large amounts does it become dangerous. Hydrogen bomb explosions create large amounts of radioactive fallout.

Fallout could settle anywhere. Winds could carry it to every part of the country.

YOU CAN SELDOM FEEL IT

OFTEN YOU CAN'T EVEN SEE IT

But if you are exposed to much of it long enough, it can make you seriously ill even if the radioactive particles do not settle on you.

IT COULD KILL YOU!

A mass of material between you and the particles is needed for protection.

Weather and radiological experts will estimate the path and speed of fallout after an attack. They will tell you how much time you have to protect yourself. If you don't get the word, play it safe. Seek the best available shelter if there has been a nuclear attack.

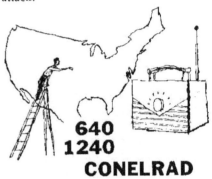

640 1240 CONELRAD

Your CONELRAD radio stations, at 640 or 1240 on your dial, will keep you informed.

Radiological monitors will measure the amount of fallout in your area. Local officials will tell you when the area is safe and when you may leave the protected area.

But the basic responsibility is yours. Listen for the instructions of your local officials. Follow them carefully.

Wherever you are—at home or away—seek the best available protection and stay there as long as you can or until advised to come out.

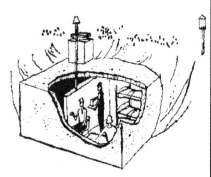

The best protection is an underground shelter with at least three feet of earth or sand above it. Two feet of concrete will give the same protection. If the shelter has an adequate door and an air filter, it will give you almost complete protection.

An ordinary house without basement probably would cut the radiation in half, if you stay on the first floor near the center of the house.

Staying in a house basement will reduce your exposure to about 1/10 the outside exposure. If you can sandbag the basement windows, there will be a further reduction.

If you arrange a basement refuge, with a mass of material around and above you, as shown, you can reduce your exposure to about 1/100 of the outside exposure.

Large buildings—apartment or office buildings—give good protection. Their masonry or concrete construction generally makes it harder for radiation to get through. Basements, inside rooms, or corridors are safest.

Outdoors, a culvert that can be blocked off at the ends will furnish protection. A trench or ditch also will protect you if it can be covered quickly with three feet of earth or other heavy materials.

REMEMBER

BE PREPARED

The more dense material you put between yourself and the fallout, the better protected you are. This can be earth, sand, or other material. In a pinch, it can be stacks of books, magazines, newspapers, or filing cabinets.

Determine which is the safest area in your home or place of business.

Fallout will sift into your house or shelter like dust. Stop up the doors and windows tightly.

Decide what needs to be done to it to give you the best possible protection.

Then do as much of this as you can—**NOW.**

If you want to build a basement shelter with concrete or sandbagged walls and ceiling, plans are available. Consult your local civil defense officials.

If you think you have been in a fallout area, wash yourself and your clothes thoroughly. If you can't wash your clothes and dispose of the water, leave your clothes outside.

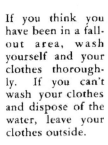

YOUR SHELTER AREA SHOULD HAVE:

SPACE

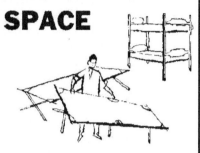

Enough to take care of your family for two weeks. Remember that you will need sleeping arrangements.

FOOD AND WATER

A two-weeks' supply of water and precooked foods for your family. Plenty of fruit juices and water. Your family's favorite canned foods can be a morale lifter. Don't forget a can opener and bottle opener.

EQUIPMENT

A battery operated radio to receive official instructions if your power fails. An extra supply of batteries. An outside antenna may be necessary.

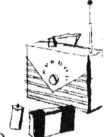

An electric light, battery operated. Extra batteries.

A first aid kit.

Blankets and bedding.

Stove for heat and cooking.

Containers for garbage and human waste.

Everything you need for a two-week's stay.

NOTE.—Supplies and equipment should be stored in your shelter area. A hurried trip can be made outside of your shelter but it should not be made unless it is absolutely necessary.

IN SUMMARY

Fallout is dangerous.

There are effective protective measures against it.

The best protection comes from three feet of earth or other heavy material between you and the fallout.

The best protection is planned and prepared in advance.

The best protection is not good enough if you can't stay in your shelter area until you are told to come out.

MP-79 / February 1979

These are
PLANS FOR EXPEDIENT
FALLOUT SHELTERS

SAVE THESE PLANS—THEY MAY SAVE YOUR LIFE

• GENERAL INFORMATION

WITHOUT PROTECTION, UNTOLD NUMBERS OF AMERICANS WOULD DIE NEEDLESSLY IN THE EVENT OF A NUCLEAR ATTACK. THE EXPEDIENT SHELTERS ILLUSTRATED IN THE FOLLOWING PAGES PROVIDE PROTECTION TO OCCUPANTS FROM THE DEADLY RADIATION OF RADIOACTIVE FALLOUT GENERATED BY A NUCLEAR DETONATION — THEIR USE CAN SAVE THE LIVES OF MILLIONS OF AMERICANS.

EVEN THOUGH THE ILLUSTRATED SHELTERS ARE VERY AUSTERE, THERE ARE A NUMBER OF THINGS THAT CAN BE DONE TO IMPROVE THEIR HABITABILITY AFTER THEY HAVE BEEN BUILT. WITH THE USE OF A LITTLE INGENUITY AND EFFORT, THE SHELTERS CAN BE MADE MORE COMFORTABLE. SOME OF THE THINGS THAT CAN BE DONE ARE :

• CONSTRUCT SEATS, HAMMOCKS, OR BUNKS.

• COVER THE FLOOR WITH BOARDS, PINE BOUGHS OR LOGS AND DRAPE SHEETS OR MATERIAL OVER THE EARTH WALLS.

• PROVIDE SAFE, DEPENDABLE LIGHT.

• FOR HOT WEATHER, CONSTRUCT THE EXPEDIENT AIR VENTILATION PUMP.

• FOR COOKING, CONSTRUCT THE EXPEDIENT COOK STOVE FOR USE IN THE ENTRY-WAY. IN COLD WEATHER, SEAL THE ENTRANCE AND USE THE STOVE FOR HEATING THE SHELTER AREA. BE SURE VENTILATION IS PROVIDED WHENEVER THE STOVE IS USED.

• STORE SHELTER SUPPLIES IN ENTRYWAY FOR MORE LIVING SPACE. COVER ALL OPEN CONTAINERS. RADIATION WILL NOT DAMAGE THESE SUPPLIES.

HUMANS MUST HAVE WATER AND FOOD TO LIVE. WHEN PEOPLE ARE TO LIVE IN A SHELTER FOR A WEEK OR TWO, SUFFICIENT FOOD AND SUPPLIES MUST BE PROVIDED FOR THE OCCUPANTS. THE MINIMUM NECESSITIES ARE:

• WATER — MINIMUM REQUIREMENTS (DEPENDENT UPON TEMPERATURE — LESS IN COLD WEATHER, MORE IN WARMER) WILL BE FROM ONE QUART TO ONE GALLON PER PERSON PER DAY. STORAGE CAN BE ACCOMPLISHED BY USING DISINFECTED METAL OR PLASTIC TRASH CANS OR BOXES LINED WITH STRONG POLYETHYLENE FILM OR STRONG PLASTIC BAGS. FOR PURITY, EIGHT DROPS (ONE TEASPOON OF A 5¼% CHLORINE SOLUTION (e.g., CLOROX) SHOULD BE MIXED INTO EACH 5 GALLONS OF WATER.

• FOOD — ALL FOOD SHOULD REQUIRE NO REFRIGERATION AND SHOULD BE BROUGHT TO THE SHELTER IN AIRTIGHT TINS OR BOTTLES. UNDER SHELTER CONDITIONS, PEOPLE WILL REQUIRE ABOUT HALF AS MUCH FOOD AS USUAL. FOODS SHOULD HAVE A HIGH NUTRITIONAL VALUE AND A MINIMAL AMOUNT OF BULK (i.e., CANNED MEATS — FRUITS — VEGETABLES, DRIED CEREALS, HARD CANDY, ETC.)

• SANITATION — A METAL CONTAINER WITH A TIGHT-FITTING LID FOR USE AS A TOILET WITH WHICH PLASTIC BAGS CAN BE USED. TOILET PAPER, SOAP, TOWELS, SANITARY ITEMS AND A QUANTITY OF STRONG PLASTIC BAGS WILL BE NEEDED.

• MEDICAL SUPPLIES — A WELL-STOCKED FIRST-AID KIT COMPARABLE TO WHAT IS USUALLY KEPT AT HOME. TAKE SPECIAL MEDICINES FOR INFANTS AND OTHERS AND A GOOD FIRST-AID HANDBOOK.

• CLOTHING AND BEDDING — SEVERAL CHANGES OF CLEAN CLOTHING, ESPECIALLY SOCKS AND UNDERCLOTHING — DEPENDENT UPON THE WEATHER, BLANKETS, PILLOWS AND SLEEPING BAGS MAY ALSO BE NEEDED.

• PORTABLE RADIO — LASTLY, BUT HARDLY LEAST IMPORTANT, A PORTABLE RADIO WITH FRESH AND EXTRA BATTERIES. RADIO STATION BROADCASTS WILL ADVISE YOU WHEN IT IS SAFE TO ABANDON THE SHELTER AND ALSO PROVIDE YOU WITH OTHER IMPORTANT EMERGENCY INFORMATION.

1

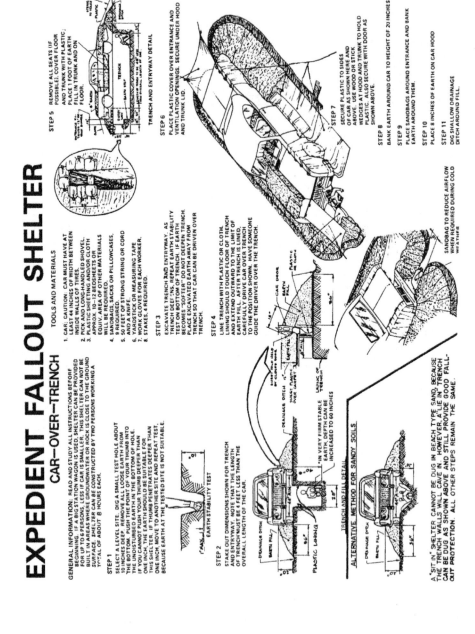

EXPEDIENT FALLOUT SHELTER

TILT-UP DOORS AND EARTH

GENERAL INFORMATION

READ AND STUDY ALL INSTRUCTIONS BEFORE STARTING TO BUILD. THE LOCATION SELECTED FOR THIS SHELTER SHOULD BE LEVEL OR GENTLY SLOPING DOWN AND AWAY FROM THE MASONRY WALL. A THREE PERSON SHELTER CAN BE CONSTRUCTED BY THREE PEOPLE WORKING A TOTAL OF 6 HOURS EACH.

STEP 1

LAY OUT THE TRENCH AND EARTH NOTCH WIDTHS, AS DIMENSIONED ON THE SECTION BELOW, ADJACENT TO A MASONRY WALL. DETERMINE THE LENGTH OF TRENCH AND NOTCH BY ALLOWING ONE DOOR WIDTH OF LENGTH PER PERSON TO BE SHELTERED.

STEP 2

EXCAVATE TRENCH AND EARTH NOTCH. PLACE EXCAVATED EARTH OUTSIDE SHELTER LIMITS FOR LATER USE.

STEP 3

REMOVE DOOR KNOBS FROM ALL DOORS. PLACE DOUBLE LAYER OF DOORS IN NOTCH AND AGAINST WALL AS SHOWN IN SKETCH. NAIL 1 x 6 BOARD TO DOOR EDGES AT ENTRANCE TO SERVE AS EARTH STOP. AFTER ATTACHING PLASTIC ENTRANCE COVER AS SHOWN, OR BUILD RETAINING WALL OF SANDBAGS IN LIEU OF BOARD. PLACE ONE DOOR ON EDGE LENGTHWISE AS THE END CLOSURE.

STEP 4

PLACE ONE END OF THE ROLLED UP WATERPROOFING MATERIAL UNDER THE TOP EDGE OF THE DOORS BEFORE EARTH FILL IS PLACED. BEGIN PLACEMENT OF EARTH FILL ON DOORS, COVER THE EARTH FILL WITH WATERPROOFING MATERIAL, SECURING IT WITH EARTH AT TOP AND BOTTOM TO PREVENT IT FROM BLOWING AWAY.

STEP 5

CONSTRUCT ENTRANCE — FILL "SANDBAG PILLOW CASES" WITH EARTH TAKEN FROM THE TRENCH AND STACK TO DIMENSIONS SHOWN. AFTER DOORS ARE IN PLACE, PLASTIC OR POLYETHYLENE WATERPROOFING MATERIAL ENTRANCE COVER SHOULD BE IN PLACE BEFORE EARTH FILL IS PUT ON THE DOORS.

TOOLS AND MATERIALS

1. TOOLS: PICK, SHOVEL, HAMMER, SAW, SCREWDRIVER, KNIFE, YARDSTICK.
2. SANDBAGS, PILLOWCASES OR PLASTIC GARBAGE BAGS – AT LEAST 39.
3. LUMBER: 1" x 6" PIECE 7'LONG (OR 20 MORE SANDBAGS) FOR EARTH FILL STOP AT ENTRANCE EDGE OF DOORS.
4. ROPE OR CORD TO TIE SANDBAGS.
5. DOORS: TWO LAYERS FOR LENGTH OF SHELTER PLUS ONE FOR END CLOSURE. (EXAMPLE: 7 DOORS FOR 3 PERSON SHELTER).
6. NAILS: 8 penny (2½" LONG), ABOUT 10 TO NAIL EARTH STOP TO DOOR EDGES AT ENTRANCE.
7. PLASTIC OR POLYETHYLENE (WATERPROOFING MATERIAL) TO COVER DOUBLE LAYER OF DOORS PLUS ENTRANCE.
8. WORK GLOVES FOR EACH WORKER.

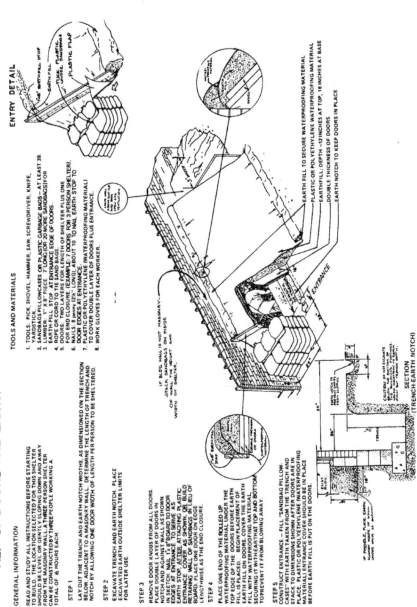

ENTRY DETAIL

PLASTIC FLAP

EARTH FILL

EARTH FILL TO SECURE WATERPROOFING MATERIAL
PLASTIC OR POLYETHYLENE WATERPROOFING MATERIAL
EARTHFILL; DEPTH –12 INCHES AT TOP, 18 INCHES AT BASE
DOUBLE THICKNESS OF DOORS
EARTH NOTCH TO KEEP DOORS IN PLACE

IF BLDG. WALL IS NOT MASONRY — STACK SANDBAGS ON INSIDE OF WALL, THE HEIGHT AND WIDTH OF SHELTER.

SECTION
(TRENCH-EARTH NOTCH)

ENTRANCE

EXPEDIENT FALLOUT SHELTER

ABOVE-GROUND DOOR-COVERED SHELTER

GENERAL INFORMATION

THE ABOVE-GROUND DOOR COVERED SHELTER IS DESIGNED FOR AREAS WHERE BELOW-GROUND SHELTERS ARE IMPRACTICAL BECAUSE THE GROUNDWATER TABLE OR BEDROCK IS CLOSE TO THE GROUND SURFACE. THIS SHELTER CAN BE BUILT BY FOUR PERSONS WORKING A TOTAL OF 10 HOURS EACH.

READ AND STUDY ALL INSTRUCTIONS BEFORE STARTING TO BUILD. IF DOOR WIDTHS MEASURE LESS THAN 32 INCHES, USE A COMBINATION OF DOORS TO PROVIDE A MINIMUM OF 32 INCHES OF DOOR WIDTH PER PERSON.

STEP 1

SELECT A SHELTER LOCATION WHERE THERE IS LITTLE OR NO CHANCE OF RAINWATER PONDING ON THE GROUND SURFACE. STAKE OUT SHELTER. REMOVE DOOR KNOBS. ALLOW 1 DOOR FOR EACH PERSON PLUS 1 DOOR FOR ENTRY EXIT AT END. LIMIT IS 8 PERSONS PER SHELTER.

DOORS (32" WIDE) 1 PER PERSON PLUS 1 FOR EXIT/ENTRY.

STEP 2

SET UP DOORS AS FORMS AROUND WHICH EARTH-FILLED ROLLS WILL BE PLACED. NAIL ONLY TOP BRACES. NAILS MUST BE REMOVED LATER. BRACE ALL CORNERS, CENTER, TOP AND BOTTOM OF EACH DOOR.

22 INCH OFFSET

CUT-OUT SECTION TO SHOW INSIDE OF EARTH ROLLS.

STEP 3

BEGIN TO PLACE EARTH FILLED ROLLS AGAINST DOOR FORMS. TO FORM EARTH ROLLS, SEE EARTH-FILLED ROLL DETAIL BOTTOM OF PAGE.

EARTH-FILLED ROLL DETAIL

1. PLACE 2 FT OF SHEET ON GROUND AND TEMPORARILY DRAPE REMAINDER OF SHEET ON DOOR
2. PLACE EARTH ON SHEET – SHAPE AS SHOWN.
3. FOLD SHEET OVER SHAPED EARTH.
4. PLACE EARTH ONTO SHEET AT NARROW TRENCH.
5. FOLD SHEET TO FORM EARTH HOOK. EARTH HOOK WILL ANCHOR SHEET.
6. REPEAT TO FORM NEXT EARTH-FILLED ROLL.

PROVIDE 4-6" DIA. PIPE FOR VENTILATION.

SHEET
EARTH HOOK
ROLL
BRACE
DOOR
EARTH FILLED ROLLS

STEP 4

DIG 14" DEEP, 36" WIDE TRENCH INSIDE SHELTER. EARTH CAN BE USED TO FORM SIDE EARTH FILLED ROLLS. TRENCH CAN BE MADE UP TO 3 FEET DEEP IF CONDITIONS PERMIT.

STEP 5

MOUND EARTH AGAINST THE EARTH-FILLED ROLLS AS SHOWN. CONTINUE PLACING EARTH AND SHEETS TO FORM EARTH-FILLED ROLLS.

STEP 6

KEEP HEIGHT OF EARTH ABOUT EQUAL ON BOTH SIDEWALLS AS ROLLS ARE FORMED. AFTER SIDEWALLS HAVE REACHED PLANNED HEIGHT, REMOVE BRACES AND DOOR FORMS. USE SAME DOOR FORMS TO CONSTRUCT ENDWALLS WITH EARTH FILLED ROLLS. PROVIDE EXIT/ENTRY AT END AS SHOWN.

STEP 7

REMOVE DOOR FORMS FROM ENDWALLS. POSITION ROOF DOORS IN THEIR FINAL POSITION. PLACE ENTRY/EXIT PLACE FRAME FOR DOOR OVER ENTRY/EXIT. PLACE WATERPROOFING MATERIAL ON DOORS.

SLOPE TO DRAIN

14 INCHES OR MORE

FOLD WATERPROOFING MATERIAL UNDER HIGHER EDGE OF DOOR TO KEEP IT FROM SLIPPING.

STEP 8

PLACE 18 INCHES OF EARTH ON TOP OF SHELTER. IN HOT WEATHER CONSTRUCT A SHELTER VENTILATION AIR PUMP. SEE AIR PUMP DETAILS ON LAST PAGE.

PLAN VIEW OF SHELTER (4 PERSON) (LOOKING DOWN)

36"-WIDE TRENCH

DOORS OR DOOR COVERED ROOF

EDGE OF MOUNDED EARTH

PILLOWCASE SANDBAGS TO IMPROVE RADIATION SHIELDING AT DOORWAY

ENTRY FRAME

SUPPORT FOR DOOR OVER DOORWAY

EDGE OF TRENCH LINE

EARTH-FILLED ROLL, END WALLS

NOTE: IF TRENCHING IS IMPRACTICAL HEIGHTEN WALLS BY USING ADDITIONAL EARTH ROLLS.

TOOLS AND MATERIALS

1. Doors as indicated.
2. Pick or Mattock and Shovel.
3. Two Buckets or Large Cans to Carry Earth.
4. Tape Measure, Yardstick or Ruler.
5. Saw, Axe or Hatchet.
6. Hammer and at least 20 Nails – 2½" long.
7. At least 4 Double Bed Sheets for Each Person to be Sheltered.
8. Pillowcases and Rainproofing Materials such as Plastic or Polyethylene.
9. Work Gloves for Each Worker.
10. Lumber for use as Temporary Braces and for Entry/Exit Frame.

ENTRY/EXIT FRAME

SIDE SUPPORT
BOTTOM BRACE
ABOUT 22 INCHES WIDE TO FIT ENTRY

USE 2" x 4" BOARDS. SIZE TO FIT ENTRYWAY OPENING AND INSTALL AFTER ENTRY IS COMPLETED.

EXPEDIENT FALLOUT SHELTER
LOG—COVERED TRENCH SHELTER

GENERAL INFORMATION

THIS SHELTER IS DESIGNED FOR AREAS WHERE THE DEPTH BELOW THE GROUND SURFACE TO HARD ROCK OR GROUNDWATER IS BELOW THE BOTTOM OF THE TRENCH. ALSO, THE EARTH MUST BE SUFFICIENTLY FIRM AND STABLE SO THAT THE TRENCH SIDEWALLS WILL NOT CAVE IN. IN ADDITION, ADEQUATE SMALL TREES THAT CAN BE CUT FOR LOGS MUST BE AVAILABLE IN THE IMMEDIATE AREA. THIS EXPEDIENT SHELTER (PERSON CAPACITY) CAN BE BUILT BY 4 PEOPLE WORKING A TOTAL OF 12 HOURS EACH. AFTER INITIAL COMPLETION, THE SHELTER CAN BE ENLARGED TO A WIDTH OF 5 FT.—6 IN. AND DEEPENED TO 6 FT. HOWEVER, 9—FT LOGS MUST BE USED IN PLACE OF 7—FT LOGS AND THE BURIED ROOF MUST BE LARGE ENOUGH TO COVER THE WIDENED SHELTER DURING THE INITIAL CONSTRUCTION.

STEP 1

CLEAR AREA OF BRUSH AND TALL GRASS. LAYOUT SHELTER AS SHOWN BELOW.

STEP 2

BEGIN EXCAVATING THE TRENCH. PLACE EXCAVATED EARTH AT LEAST 3 FEET BEYOND THE EDGE OF TRENCH SO THAT THE ROOF LOGS CAN LATER BE PLACED OVER THE TRENCH.

STEP 3

AS THE TRENCH EXCAVATION PROGRESSES, SOME WORKERS SHOULD BEGIN CUTTING LOGS TO THE LENGTH AND SIZE AS SHOWN ON THE ILLUSTRATIONS.

STEP 4

PLACE LOGS OVER TRENCH. POSITION TIES FOR BED SHEET CHAIRS OR HAMMOCKS. PLACE NEWSPAPER OR OTHER MATERIAL AS INDICATED OVER BURIED ROOF. PLACE EARTH FILL AND BURIED ROOF.

SECTION A—A

STEP 5

CONSTRUCT CANOPIES OVER THE OPENINGS

TOOLS AND MATERIALS

1. SAW AND/OR AXE.
2. PICK OR MATTOCK.
3. LONG-HANDLED SHOVELS.
4. RAINPROOFING MATERIAL (PLASTIC OR POLYETHYLENE 25 SQUARE YARDS. FOR EACH PERSON ABOVE 4, ADD 2 SQ. YDS.
5. 50 FEET OF STRONG STRING OR CORD AND A KNIFE.
6. TAPE MEASURE OR YARD STICK.
7. AT LEAST 8 PILLOW CASES AND/OR SANDBAGS.
8. WORK GLOVES.
9. BED SHEETS FOR USE AS "CHAIRS" OR "HAMMOCKS" — 1 PER PERSON PLUS AT LEAST 15 FEET OF STRONG ROPE OR CORD PER BED SHEET
10. 15 POUNDS OF NEWSPAPERS TO PLACE OVER ROOF LOGS TO KEEP EARTH FROM FALLING THROUGH CRACKS BETWEEN LOGS.

APPROX. NO. OF POLES REQ'D.		
45 –	7' LONG	4" DIA.
10 –	5' "	4" "

PICTORIAL VIEW OF LOG COVERED TRENCH SHELTER WITH PART OF THE ROOF CUT AWAY TO SHOW THE RAINPROOF BURIED ROOF.

PLAN VIEW OF TOP OF SHELTER

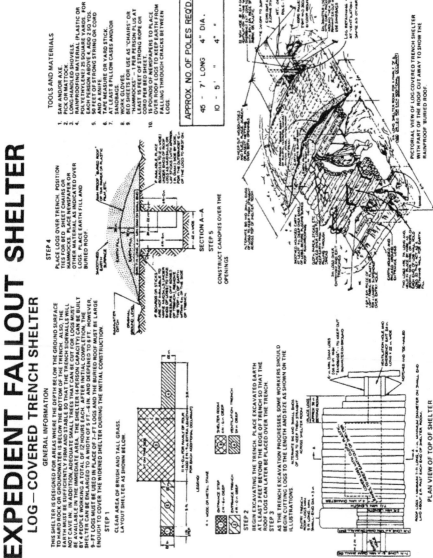

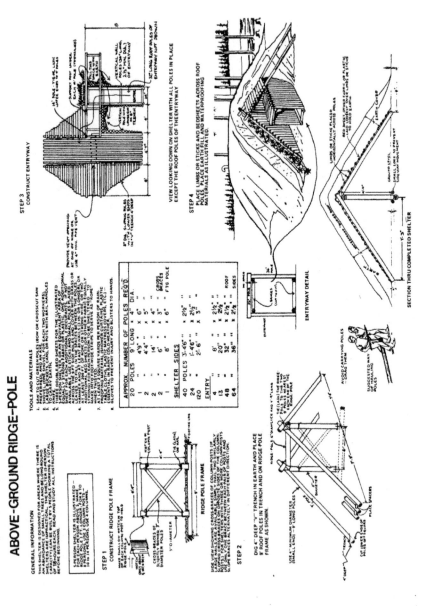

EXPEDIENT FALLOUT SHELTER

ABOVE-GROUND RIDGE-POLE

EXPEDIENT FALLOUT SHELTER
CRIB-WALLED SHELTER(ABOVE GROUND)

GENERAL INFORMATION

THIS SHELTER CAN BE CONSTRUCTED IN AREAS WHERE THERE IS AN ABUNDANCE OF SMALL TREES. THE APPROXIMATE TIME AND EFFORT REQUIRED TO BUILD THIS SHELTER (CAP) FOR 5 IS 2 PERSONS WORKING 24 TO 48 HOURS. READ AND STUDY ALL INSTRUCTIONS BEFORE STARTING TO BUILD.

TOOLS & MATERIALS
(FOR 5 PERSON CAPACITY)

1. SAW AND/OR AXE TO CUT TREE POLES.
2. SHOVELS (ONE FOR EACH TWO WORKERS).
3. LARGE CANS, BUCKETS AND/OR POTS WITH BAIL HANDLES TO CARRY EARTH.
4. KNIFE OR SCISSORS.
5. AT LEAST 280 FT. OF STRONG WIRE OR 300 FT. OF 3/16" OR LARGER CORD OR ROPE TO TIE OR TEAR INTO 1,000 WIDE STRIPS TO SERVE AS ROPE WHEN SLIGHTLY TWISTED. FOR EACH.

ADDITIONAL PERSON ABOVE 5, 20 FT. OF ROPE.
6. AT LEAST 30 SQUARE YARDS OF RAINPROOF MATERIAL SUCH AS SHEETS OF PLASTIC OR CA. VASES SHOWER CURTAINS, TABLECLOTHS, ETC.
7. POLES OF OTHER SMALLER MATERIAL FOR ROOF.
8. BLUE LEVEL OTHER PLASTIC MATERIAL COVER, CA. CLOTH OR PLASTIC AT LEAST AS WIDE AS THE BED GROOVES.
9. GLOVES TO PROTECT HANDS FROM INJURY AND BLISTERS, FOR EACH WORKER.
10. 15 POUNDS OF NEWSPAPER FOR ROOF COVER.

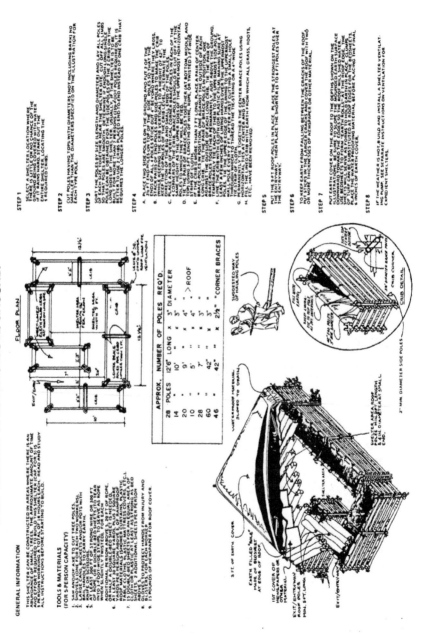

FLOOR PLAN

APPROX. NUMBER OF POLES REQ'D.			
28 POLES	12'6" LONG	x 3" DIAMETER	
14 "	10' "	x 4" "	
20 "	9' "	x 4" "	} ROOF
10 "	5' "	x 4" "	
28 "	7' "	x 3" "	
60 "	42" "	x 3" "	
46 "	42" "	x 2½" "	"CORNER BRACES"

SUGGESTED WAY OF HAULING POLES

CRIB DETAIL

STEP 1
SELECT A SHELTER LOCATION WHERE THERE WILL BE SUFFICIENT SHADE FOR THE GROUND BEING COVERED WITH WATER. IF FEASIBLE, DEVELOP A ROUTE AT THE NEAREST HORIZONTAL LOCATING THE 5 REQUIRED CRIBS.

STEP 2
CUT POLES HAVING TOPS WITH DIAMETERS (NOT INCLUDING BARK) NO SMALLER THAN THE DIAM. OF EACH SPECIFIED ON THE ILLUSTRATION FOR EACH TYPE POLE.

STEP 3
SPACE CRIBS TOGETHER THE LENGTH AND DIAMETER) AND LAY ALL POLES OF SAME LENGTH AND SIZE IN ONE AREA. THEN THERE WILL BE NO CONFUSION WHEN YOU NEED A PARTICULAR LENGTH AND DIAMETER POLE. SET CRIBS AS SMOOTH. FLAT AND LEVEL AS POSSIBLE. THE CRIB SIDE POLES ARE LONG ENOUGH LONG ENOUGH. OF THE FLOOR THE SHELTER IS TO BE BUILT ON. IF THE CRIBS ARE OF WOOD, CRIBS SUCH THAT CRIBS PLACED END TO END INSTEAD OF ONE CRIB THAT IS REQUIRED TO USE 2 CRIBS PLACED END TO END INSTEAD OF ONE CRIB THAT

STEP 4
A. PLACING TWO SIDE POLES ON THE GROUND AS FAR APART AS THE 20 FT LONG POLES ON TOP OF THE SIDE POLES SO THAT THE CRIB.
B. STACK PAIRS OF TIED POLES AND SIDE POLES WHERE THEY CROSS. THE POLES OF THE CORNERS OF THE CRIB VERTICALLY TO A HEIGHT OF 4 FT. TO NEED THE CORNER POLE BIG AND SMALL ENDS.
C. DIRECT EACH PAIR OF THE BIG AND SMALL ENDS OF THE POLES.
D. ALTERNATE AS YOU LAY EACH PAIR, BRACE POLES SHOULD BE CUT OFF AT THE 4 CORNERS OF THE CRIB. BRACE POLES SHOULD BE CUT OFF AT THE POLES TO WHICH THEY ARE TIED. USE THREE (AT BOTTOM, MIDDLE AND TOP) IF YOU USE LENGTHS OF WIRE, ROPE, OR TWISTED, IF WIDE.
E. BRACE CRIBS MORE THAN 2 FT LONG. PLACE A PAIR OF CENTER LONG CRIB. TIE THE POLES AT GROUND ABOVE THE GROUND. POLES.
F. LINE THE CRIB WITH CLOTH (OR PLASTIC FILM) MAKING DURABLE POLES. TIE THE UPPER EDGE OF THE LINING TO THE UPPERMOST POLES. TIE THE UPPER EDGE OF THE LINING TO THE UPPERMOST THROUGH WHICH TO THREAD THE TIE LINE OR A SMALL COVER.
G. PERMANENTLY TIE TOGETHER THE CENTER BRACE POLES USING.
H. FILL THE LINED CRIB WITH EARTH FROM WHICH ALL GRASS, ROOTS, ETC., HAVE BEEN REMOVED.

STEP 5
PUT THE 8 FT ROOF POLES IN PLACE. PLACE THE STRONGEST POLES AT THE ENTRYWAY. THEN PLACE THE SHORTER 8 TO 8 FT POLES OVER THE ENTRYWAY.

STEP 6
TO KEEP EARTH FROM FALLING BETWEEN THE CRACKS OF THE ROOF, COVER THE ROOF WITH ANY AVAILABLE PIECES OF EARTH SURFACE OR MORE THICKNESSES OF NEWSPAPER OR OTHER MATERIAL.

STEP 7
PUT EARTH COVER ON THE ROOF TO THE DEPTHS SHOWN ON THE DOWNWARD WORK DOWN THE ROOF SO THAT THE EARTH SURFACE COVER. THE BEDSHEETS TO FORM (EARTH ROLLS) AT THE ROOF EDGE. THE USE OF POLES OR EARTH FILLED ROLLS AT THE ROOF EDGE, THE PLACE OF A CAN BE SUBSTITUTED AT ROOF EDGES FOR THE EARTH BY, PLACE IT ON CLOTH OR OTHER MATERIAL BEFORE PLACING THE FINAL 6 INCHES OF EARTH COVER.

STEP 8
IF THE WEATHER IS HOT, BUILD AND INSTALL A SHELTER VENTILAT. INCH PUMP. SEE THE SEPARATE INSTRUCTIONS ON VENTILATION FOR EXPEDIENT SHELTERS.

EXPEDIENT FALLOUT SHELTER

AIR VENTILATION PUMP—EMERGENCY LAMP—BUCKET STOVE

ALL EXPEDIENT SHELTERS ARE DESIGNED TO PROVIDE FOR SOME NATURAL VENTILATION. IN VERY HOT WEATHER, ADDITIONAL VENTILATION MAY BE REQUIRED TO PROVIDE A LIVABLE TEMPERATURE. CONSTRUCTION OF AN AIR PUMP THAT CAN PROVIDE ADDITIONAL VENTILATION IS ILLUSTRATED BELOW.

STUDY ALL INSTRUCTIONS BEFORE STARTING CONSTRUCTION

STEP 1 AIR PUMP

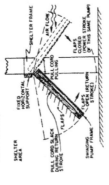

THE AIR PUMP OPERATES BY BEING SWUNG LIKE A PENDULUM. IT IS HINGED AT THE TOP OF ITS SWINGING FRAME. IT IS SWUNG BY PULLING ON AN ATTACHED CORD. THE FLAPS ARE FREE TO ALSO SWING AND WHEN THEY ARE IN THE CLOSED POSITION, AIR IS PUSHED THROUGH THE OPENING THAT THE PUMP IS ATTACHED TO.

SHELTER AREA
FIXED HORIZONTAL SUPPORT
SHELTER FRAME
AIR FLOW
FLAPS CLOSED (POWER STROKE)
FLAPS OPEN (RETURN STROKE)
PULL CORD SLACK DURING RETURN STROKE
FLAPS
SWINGING PUMP FRAME
PULL CORD PULLING

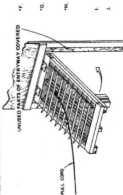

UNUSED PARTS OF ENTRYWAY COVERED
PULL CORD

TO OBTAIN MAXIMUM EFFICIENCY AND MOVE THE LARGEST AMOUNT OF AIR, THE UNUSED PORTIONS OF THE ENTRYWAY SHOULD BE COVERED WITH WOOD, PLASTIC, CLOTH, STIFF PAPER OR SIMILAR MATERIALS.

STEP 2 MATERIALS AND TOOLS NEEDED TO CONSTRUCT AN AIR PUMP

(MATERIALS SIZED FOR A 36-INCH BY 29-INCH PUMP)
LUMBER SIZES CAN BE ALTERED, DEPENDING ON AVAILABILITY.

* A. LUMBER

SIZE	QUANTITY	SIZE	QUANTITY
1" X 7" X 36"	2	1" X 2" X 33"	2
1" X 1" X 36"	1	1" X 1" X 32"	1
1" X 2" X 29"	2	1" X 4" X 36"	1

B. ONE PAIR ORDINARY DOOR OR CABINET BUTT HINGES, OR METAL STRAP HINGES, OR IMPROVISED HINGES MADE OF LEATHER, WOVEN STRAPS, CORDS OR FOUR HOOK & EYE SCREWS WHICH CAN BE JOINED TO FORM TWO HINGES.

C. 24 NAILS ABOUT 2" LONG, PLUS SCREWS FOR HINGES.

*D. POLYETHYLENE FILM, 3 TO 4 MILS THICK, OR PLASTIC DROP CLOTH, OR RAINCOAT-TYPE FABRIC, OR STRONG HEAVY PAPER — 10 RECTANGULAR-SHAPED PIECES, 30" X 5¾".

*E. 30" OF SMOOTH, STRAIGHT WIRE FOR USE AS FLAP PIVOT WIRES — (ABOUT AS THICK AS COAT-HANGER WIRE) OR CUT FROM 10 WIRE COAT HANGERS, OR 35' OF NYLON STRING (COAT-HANGER WIRE THICKNESS).

*F. 20 SMALL STAPLES, OR SMALL NAILS, OR 60 TACKS TO ATTACH FLAP PIVOT WIRES TO WOOD FRAME.

*G. 30" OF ¾" TO 1" WIDE PRESSURE-SENSITIVE WATERPROOF TAPE THAT DOES NOT STRETCH, OR USE NEEDLE AND THREAD TO SEW HEM TUNNELS TO THE FLAPS.

*H. FOR FLAP STOPS, 150 FT OF LIGHT STRING, STRONG THREAD, OR THIN SMOOTH WIRE. 90 TACKS OR SMALL NAILS TO ATTACH FLAP STOPS TO THE WOOD FRAME, OR FLAP STOPS CAN BE TIED TO THE FRAME.

I. 10 FEET OF CORD FOR THE PULL CORD.

J. DESIRABLE TOOLS: HAMMER, SAW, WIRECUTTER-PLIERS, SCREWDRIVER, SMALL DRILL, SCISSORS, KNIFE, YARDSTICK, AND PENCIL.

* Items must be sized or adjusted to fit opening into which airpump is to be placed.

STEP 3 HOW TO CONSTRUCT THE AIR PUMP

A. CUT LUMBER AND ASSEMBLE FRAME AS SHOWN

NOTE: DIMENSIONS SHOWN FOR FRAME MAY HAVE TO BE ADJUSTED TO FIT OPENINGS IN A SHELTER.

BACK SIDE OF FRAME

B. COMPLETE FRAME AND ATTACH HINGES. IF DRILL IS NOT AVAILABLE TO DRILL SCREW HOLES TO ATTACH HINGES, USE A NAIL TO MAKE THE HOLES.

NOTE HINGES ARE ON THE FRONT SIDE OF FRAME

COMPLETING THE FRAME.

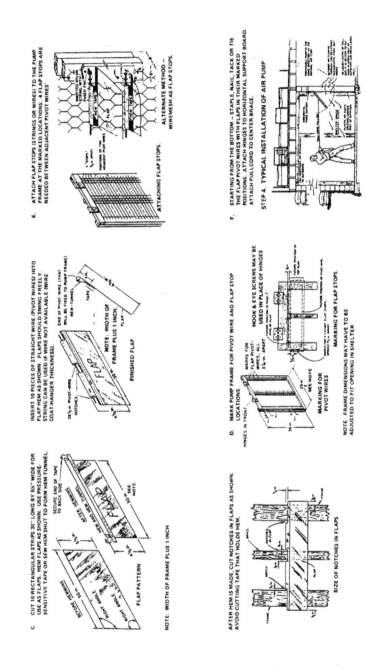

HOW TO CONSTRUCT THE AIR PUMP (CONT'D)

C. CUT 10 RECTANGULAR STRIPS 30" LONG BY 5¼" WIDE FOR USE AS FLAPS. HEM FLAPS AS SHOWN. USE PRESSURE-SENSITIVE TAPE OR SEW HEM SHUT TO FORM HEM TUNNEL.

FLAP PATTERN

NOTE: WIDTH OF FRAME PLUS 1 INCH

INSERT 10 PIECES OF STRAIGHT WIRE (PIVOT WIRES) INTO FLAP HEM AS SHOWN. FLAPS SHOULD SWING FREELY. STRING CAN BE USED IF WIRE NOT AVAILABLE (WIRE COAT-HANGER THICKNESS).

FINISHED FLAP

NOTE: WIDTH OF FRAME PLUS 1 INCH.

E. ATTACH FLAP STOPS (STRINGS OR WIRES) TO THE PUMP FRAME AT THE MARKED LOCATIONS. 4 FLAP STOPS ARE NEEDED BETWEEN ADJACENT PIVOT WIRES.

ATTACHING FLAP STOPS.

ALTERNATE METHOD — WIREMESH AS FLAP STOPS.

AFTER HEM IS MADE, CUT NOTCHES IN FLAPS AS SHOWN. AVOID CUTTING TAPE THAT HOLDS HEM.

SIZE OF NOTCHES IN FLAPS

D. MARK PUMP FRAME FOR PIVOT WIRE AND FLAP STOP LOCATIONS

MARKING FOR PIVOT WIRES

HOOK & EYE SCREWS MAY BE USED IN PLACE OF HINGES

MARKING FOR FLAP STOPS.

NOTE: FRAME DIMENSIONS MAY HAVE TO BE ADJUSTED TO FIT OPENING IN SHELTER

F. STARTING FROM THE BOTTOM — STAPLE, NAIL, TACK OR TIE THE FLAP PIVOT WIRES WITH FLAPS IN THEIR MARKED POSITIONS. ATTACH HINGES TO HORIZONTAL SUPPORT BOARD. ATTACH PULLCORD TO CENTER BRACE.

STEP 4. TYPICAL INSTALLATION OF AIR PUMP

IX

EMERGENCY LAMP

THIS TYPE OF LAMP WILL PROVIDE LIGHT FOR USE IN EXPEDIENT SHELTERS – THE LAMP WILL BURN SLOWLY CONSUMING ABOUT 3 OUNCES OF COOKING OIL IN 24 HOURS.

WARNING
DO NOT USE KEROSENE, DIESEL FUEL, OR GASOLINE — USE ONLY OILS OF THE KIND FOUND IN THE KITCHEN.

LOOP TO HANG LAMP

TO LIGHT LAMP, FIRST MAKE MATCH LONGER BY TAPING OR TYING IT TO A STICK.

LIGHT WIRE

CLEAN GLASS JAR FREE OF LABELS

FLAME FROM END OF WICK IS JUST ABOVE OIL SURFACE

A FINE WIRE TIED IN ITS CENTER AROUND THE NAILS, WITH THE ENDS OF THE WIRE WOUND IN OPPOSITE DIRECTIONS AROUND THE COTTON-STRING-WICK. USE COTTON THAT IS SLIGHTLY LESS THAN 1/8-IN. IN DIAMETER. USE WINDOW SCREEN WIRE OR OTHER EQUALLY FINE WIRE.

ATTACH ALUMINUM FOIL 2/3 AROUND JAR AND UNDER ITS BOTTOM AND TO WIRES TO ACT AS A REFLECTOR.

FILL JAR NO MORE THAN HALF-FULL WITH COOKING OIL.

BENT NAIL, TIED OVER TOP OF ANOTHER BENT NAIL, SO THE BASE WILL NOT ROCK.

USE NAILS ABOUT 1/4-IN. SHORTER THAN THE DIAMETER OF JAR.

WIRE-STIFFENED-WICK LAMP

KEEP EXTRA WIRE AND WICK-STRING IN SHELTER.

BUCKET STOVE

THIS COMBINATION COOK-STOVE/SPACE-HEATER IS MADE USING A 10 TO 16 qt. METAL PA... SOME COAT-HANGER WIRE, AND METAL CUT FROM A LARGE JUICE OR VEGETABLE CAN. WHEN ASSEMBLED AS SHOWN, THE STOVE WILL BRING 3qts. OF WATER TO A BOIL USING AS FUEL, ABOUT 1/2 lb. OF DRY, TWISTED PAPER OR DRY WOOD. PIECES OF WOOD ABOUT 1/2 x 3/4 x 6 INCHES ARE BEST.

NOTE:
LOCATE COOK-STOVE ONLY WHERE EITHER NATURAL OR FORCED VENTILATION IS CAUSING AIR TO LEAVE THE SHELTER– DO NOT OPERATE IN A SEALED SHELTER.

TWO COAT HANGERS USED TO FORM COOK-POT SUPPORT. BEND AS SHOWN TO PRESS FIRMLY AGAINST SIDES OF BUCKET.

CUT THE DAMPER FROM A JUICE CAN. BEND THE SIDES WITH PLIERS AROUND COAT-HANGER WIRE USED TO ATTACH DAMPER TO PAIL. THIS ALLOWS IT TO MOVE UP AND DOWN.

USING A COLD CHISEL AND TIN SNIPS, CUT A 5 x 5 SQUARE HOLE IN THE PAIL. WHEN USING COLD CHISEL, PLACE PAIL OVER THE END OF A LOG TO AVOID CRUSHING THE PAIL.

ALUMINUM FOIL PLACED IN BOTTOM OF PAIL AND WRAPPED HALFWAY AROUND IT REFLECTS HEAT BOTH TOWARD COOK-POT AND TOWARD SHELTER AREA WHEN DEVICE IS USED AS A SPACE HEATER.

USE 4 OR 5 METAL COAT HANGERS TO FASHION A GRATE AS SHOWN

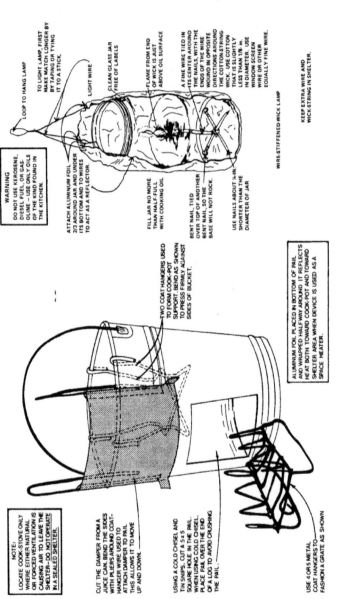

Printed in Great Britain
by Amazon

23544108R00040